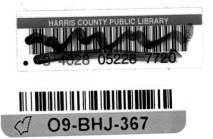
Bringing Out Their Best

Bringing Out Their Best

Values Education and Character Development Through Traditional Tales

Norma J. Livo

2003
LIBRARIES UNLIMITED
A Division of Greenwood Publishing Group, Inc.
Westport, Connecticut

LIBRARIES UNLIMITED
Teacher Ideas Press

A Division of Greenwood Publishing Group, Inc.
88 Post Road West
Westport, CT 06881
1–800–225–5800
www.lu.com

Library of Congress Cataloging-in-Publication Data

Livo, Norma J., 1929–
    Bringing out their best : values education and character development through traditional tales / Norma J. Livo.
        p. cm.
Includes bibliographical references
    ISBN 1–56308–934–3 (pbk.)
1. Tales. 2. Storytelling. 3. Social values—Study and teaching.
I. Title
GR72.L59   2003
398.2—dc21   2002155406

To George. After more than fifty-one years together, our stories demonstrate character and values. Your legacy is rich.

Contents

Introduction 1

LOVE ﾍﾙ 9

The Bamboo Princess (Japan) 11
Lovers in the Sky (China) 15
The Lovers of Spirit Lake (Native American, Iowa, USA) 18
The Parable of the Good Samaritan (New Testament,
  Christian Bible) 19
The Selkie (Scotland) 20
Thoughts About the Stories, Discussions, and Activities 22
Other Activity Ideas 24

APPRECIATION ﾍﾙ 27

The Delicious Strawberry (Zen Buddhist) 29
The Stonecutter (Japan) 30
The Wind and the Sun (Aesop) 32
The Town Mouse and the Country Mouse (Aesop) 33
Thoughts About the Stories, Discussions, and Activities 34
Other Activity Ideas 36

PERSEVERANCE ❧ 39

Robert the Bruce, the King (Scotland) 41

The Storyteller (Ethiopia) 43

The Dragon and the Prince (Poland) 45

The Singing, Soaring Lark (Germany) 51

Thoughts About the Stories, Discussions, and Activities 56

Other Activity Ideas 58

TRUSTWORTHINESS ❧ 61

The Lute Player (Russia) 63

The Wonderful Hair (Slavonic) 67

Ananzi and the Lion (Africa) 70

The Boy Who Cried Wolf (Aesop) 73

The Donkey in the Lion's Skin (Aesop) 74

The Glencoe Massacre (Scotland—A True Story) 75

The Monkey and the Dolphin (Aesop) 79

Thoughts About the Stories, Discussions, and Activities 80

Other Activity Ideas 83

SELF-DISCIPLINE ❧ 87

Tiger's Whisker (Korea) 89

The Magic Fish of Gold (Finland) 92

The Bag of Gold (Finland) 96

Thoughts About the Stories, Discussions, and Activities 99

Other Activity Ideas 101

SELF-CONFIDENCE ❧ 103

The Hummingbird (China) 105

The Fifty-First Dragon (An Original Story by Heywood Broun) 106

Seizing the Nettles (Scotland) 113

Thoughts About the Stories, Discussions, and Activities 114

Other Activity Ideas 116

COMPASSION ✤ 119

The Badger's Money (Japan) 121

Arion and His Harp (Greece) 125

The Grateful Foxes (Japan) 128

The Fox and the Horse (Germany, Brothers Grimm) 133

The Golden Lion (Italy) 135

The Deer of India (India) 141

Old Badger and Old Frog (Native American, California, USA) 144

Thoughts About the Stories, Discussions, and Activities 145

Other Activity Ideas 148

RESPONSIBILITY ✤ 151

The Little Red Hen (United States) 153

The Three Shirts of Bog Cotton (Scotland) 155

The Sage Grouse (Paiute, North America) 162

Thoughts About the Stories, Discussions, and Activities 163

Other Activity Ideas 165

COOPERATION ✤ 167

The Lion and the Mouse (Aesop) 169

Lessons from a Father (Tennessee, USA) 170

The Hunt (Aesop) 172

The Escape of the Pigeons (Persia) 173

The Great Canoe (Maori, New Zealand) 175

Stealing Fire (Native American, Oregon, USA) 178

The Crane and the Wood Grouse (Finland) 180

Long, Broad, and Sharpsight (Slavonic) 181

Thoughts About the Stories, Discussions, and Activities 190

Other Activity Ideas 193

RESPECT ❧ 195

Intelligence and Luck (Slavonic) 197

Healing Well (Scotland) 201

Two Friends (Africa) 202

The Man Who Roared (Colorado, USA) 204

Thoughts About the Stories, Discussions, and Activities 207

Other Activity Ideas 209

FAIRNESS ❧ 211

The Bagpiper and the Rats (Germany) 213

Coyote and Fox (Native American, Colorado, USA) 217

Toads and Diamonds (France) 220

Thoughts About the Stories, Discussions, and Activities 223

Other Activity Ideas 225

DEALING WITH BULLIES ❧ 227

Three Billy Goats Gruff (Norway) 229

Basket Woman (Ute, North America) 231

The Monkeys and the Grasshoppers (Hmong, Southeast Asia) 233

Jack and the Beanstalk (England) 235

David and Goliath (Old Testament, Judeo Christian Bible) 241

The Magic Knot (Peru) 243

Thoughts About the Stories, Discussions, and Activities 250

Other Activity Ideas 253

General Activity Ideas 257

Bibliography 261

Index 265

Introduction

The traditional greeting in the Masai tribe is, "And how are the children?" The traditional answer is, "All the children are well." Meaning that peace and safety prevail, that life is good and that the struggle for existence, even among a poor people, does not preclude proper care for the young.

Beginnings are important; in fact, they are the most challenging part of anything. Many times, "getting started" means creating something from raw material. Nurturing and teaching children certainly provides essential beginnings. Our children are our legacy to the world. That is why it is so important to develop their imaginations and abilities to visualize, and to provide stories that can serve as vaccination against future social pressures.

Violence in America has reached epidemic proportions and that is certainly reflected in our schools. In response, community groups and school systems throughout the country have been urging that more attention be directed to character development and values education. The dictionary defines character as "the aggregate of properties and qualities that distinguishes one person or thing from another, a trait, good qualities." For the discussion of character traits, others often refer to morals, ethics, and values.

School districts throughout our country are presently focused on traits such as perseverance, trustworthiness, self-discipline, compassion, responsibility, and respect. Some character education advocates recommend that a national character education effort should also include citizenship, fairness, punctuality, and cleanliness, as well as manners.

Educators have long held that good character and good citizenship were at the core of the mission of public education. During the 1960s and 1970s, as sensitivity toward religious and cultural diversity awakened, character education faded and educators became more reluctant to impose values on the children. They left it up to the students to sort out right from wrong. Values were considered concepts that needed to be clarified, not taught. But more recently, President George W. Bush announced during his 2000 election campaign that education is one of his top priorities, and he has called for teaching values in schools.

This trend has influenced current decision making on school efforts. Federal, state, and local education policymakers are involved in the effort. As recently as March 2001, legislation has been enacted in twenty-eight states to integrate character education into the classrooms. Another related trend in public education comes through legislation that introduces teaching units on patriotism, including, but not limited to, a discussion of the rights, privileges, and responsibilities involved in U.S. citizenship. The aftereffects of and response to September 11, 2001 continue to influence education legislation in a variety of ways.

Currently, educators say that we need to encourage civic virtues and share moral values such as honesty and caring in the schools. State congresses are enacting legislation to encourage school districts to come up with classes and programs that, for example, "cultivate honesty, respect, responsibility, courtesy, obedience to the law" and other good-citizen qualities. Some schools promote character education by demonstrating to the students that they should take responsibility for their actions, evaluate their own behavior, and solve problems.

This approach seems to follow in the wake of the Columbine School violence of the late 1990s. One thread common to the current thinking is that schools need to teach students how to work with others and to reduce school violence, as well as substance abuse, vandalism, and teen pregnancy. Bullying is one of the central issues addressed in considering values education. Character and ethics education, it is said, should be in place to help students understand their own behavior and provide a way to frame moral questions.

A local school in Denver, Colorado, has instituted a program in which "students practice organizational skills, support and interact with others, are enthusiastic about learning, take risks, accept challenges, accept responsibility for behavior, listen attentively, follow directions, stay on task and evaluate their own learning." This school encourages these basic activities as a foundation for further values education.

Character education has also been undertaken in the nonprofit sector. For example, actor Andrew Shue heads a nonprofit program, "Kindness and Justice Challenge," cofounded in 1993. It is based on values taught by

Dr. Martin Luther King Jr.: tolerance, responsibility, compassion, nonviolence, and moral courage. Their goal is to "provide the skills and opportunities to create a better school, community and world." This is just another example of the emphasis on value education for the creation of a better world.

But character education is not just the responsibility of the government or the schools. It is also the business of the family and of the individual. Truly, it is the work of the soul.

It is interesting to refer back to the thoughts of those leaders, such as Thomas Jefferson, who wrote the Constitution and the amendments, and to their belief that public education was the important link in connecting the people to the government. They believed that our country could not afford ignorance and that every citizen should be well educated. The citizens, according to Jefferson, should be trusted and should make their own choices.

It was out of these beliefs that our educational system evolved. Thus, the humanities mined the text and stories of the past and the cultural expression became what people could agree upon. This then translated into a philosophy that the humanities are the work of the soul. Under that system of thought, it was purported that people need to be exposed to literature, its ideas and thoughts, and given time to absorb the wealth of it.

Knowledge is power. Today we have amazing access to it. For instance, there are not only school, public, and professional libraries available, but also the Internet possibilities. The Internet has brought the world of knowledge to us with easy access. Again, Jefferson would say that an informed citizen must make his own choices and decisions based on the information that is available. But the amount of information available is sometimes mind-boggling. That's where the soul comes in. We must not rely on legislative decisions alone in education, but apply our own recognition of what is good and true as informed thinkers.

ABOUT STORIES

This book encourages the use of stories in developing character and the life skills imparted by strong values. Why? Stories help us remain true to ourselves on our life journeys. They link the generations and serve as maps and markers left by those who have successfully gone before us.

Stories have the power to reach within, to command emotion, to compel involvement, and to transport us into timelessness. They are a way of thinking, a primary organizer of information and ideas, the soul of a culture, and the consciousness of a people. Stories are a way in which we can know, remember, and understand.

Lately we hear many loud complaints that we have a whole generation of people who never learned morals and values. In response, storyteller Laura Simms has said, "In Africa, it is said that if you hear stories as a child, then you grow up with an inner strength born of having strong values of relatedness, respect, dignity, and ethics."

Today we certainly have immediate communication through television, cell phones, and e-mail; but are these communications of value? Do they mean anything? Recently while walking on a street in downtown Denver, I heard the fellow ahead of me with a cell phone to his ear say, "I am right in front of the building now." Was this communication full of depth, value, and importance? I think not. If we are to survive and thrive, we need deeper communication.

Television, audiotapes, and even "bedtime story" videotapes often entertain today's children. This reliance on the electronic media would suggest that bedtime cuddling, sharing a book together, and telling stories has been "improved" by or replaced with recorded "bedtime stories."

Exposure to literature should provide enjoyment and help youngsters realize its importance as a mirror of human experiences, reflecting human motives, conflicts, and values. Young story listeners should be able to identify with characters in human situations as a means of relating to others. They also should learn to appreciate the rhythms and beauty of language and develop habits of storytelling and reading that carry over into their adult lives. A story that is shared between two individuals creates a strong bond and is a powerful learning experience.

Throughout human history, folktales have given us models of behavior that is rewarded (after all, modest, well-behaved Cinderella did win the prince) and behavior that is punished (Cinderella's selfish stepsisters got their just deserts). In fact, you might say folktales are recipes for studying human motives, conflicts, and values.

One day the gods decided to create the universe. They created stars, the sun and the moon. They created the seas, mountains, flowers, trees, and clouds. They created human beings. After everything in the universe had been created, they created Truth. They weren't sure where they should place Truth. They wanted it to be somewhere where people would not find it right away. They wanted to make sure people had to search for Truth. And so, they considered putting it on the highest mountain, the farthest star, the deepest and darkest abyss or to conceal it on the secret side of the moon. Finally the gods decided to put Truth inside the human heart so peo-

ple would search throughout the universe for it and only find it when they look within.

(Traditional Far Eastern Story)

What is a story? It depends on who hears it. As listeners we all hear different things in the same story. Some of the deeper truths we are ready for, and some stories we just skim off the top. The same story can leave one listener with a smile and another with tears. And in different times of our lives, we will receive different truths from the same story. Whether we know it or not, we are all guided by voices of our ancestors—they had generations of memory in their heads.

Children are wonderful listeners and observers. They "hear" much more in stories than we give them credit for. As we get older, our expectations fill our minds and we stop trusting what we see and hear. We impart our own adult details into the stories we hear. In some ways we are ready to hear a powerful story, yet we are sometimes too full of our own preconceptions to really hear the message.

An effective storyteller is a person who has a good memory and hopes other people don't. In olden days, the real power of the wizards was their magic of words. Finns believed their old wizard Vainomoinen from the *Kalavela* epic could win battles, restore victims of battle, and solve problems with his words and songs. Imagining and believing are the only forms of magic left in the world today. The stories we hear nurture our imaginations and beliefs, and can sustain us in our lives.

It is said that through the ages there have been those who agitate and drum up the people to a cause. Then there is the warrior who goes forward and fights. The storyteller recounts events; and this is the one who survives and outlives all the others. The storyteller creates and communicates history. He gives us the shared memory that the survivors must have—otherwise their surviving would have no meaning. Memory is necessary if survival is going to be more than just a technical thing.

Of all the inanimate objects, of all people's creations, stories are the nearest to us, for they contain our very thoughts, our ambitions, our indignations, our illusions, our fidelity to truth, and our persistent leaning toward error. But most of all, stories resemble us in their precarious hold on life.

The people who can tell the best stories will shape the next century. Stories, not just facts and data, animate people and stir families, organizations, and even nations, moving them to bigger and better things. Good stories inspire. They convey knowledge, create heroes, heroines, and role models. They instill values. Our stories are simply part of creation's ongoing conversation. They are also the punctuation marks in our lives.

"Story" is a way of organizing language and thinking. It has archetypal dimensions. An archetype is a model, prototype, or pattern for the construction or recognition of other like things. In the Jungian definition, archetypal patterns are subconscious images, ideas, or patterns of thought universally present in memory in all individuals within a culture and, presumably, inherited from the ancestors of the race. Characters within stories, thematic content of stories, common patterns of story structure, and even "story" itself are archetypal. Due to this nature, there is a more profound and "real" truth in "story" than in the common reality of daily experience.

For instance, in stories, archetypes include these characters recognized for their universal traits: the youngest sister or brother (representing innocence, humility, honesty, and good), the fool (illogic and fate), the old woman/man (death), the mistreated child or stepchild, the uncaring parent or stepparent, the witch or stepmother-witch (evil), and the fearsome beast.

Animals as story characters are also important, and not simply because they are so darn cute. There is much more to it than that. Maybe it is because animals are just a bit different from real people so that the dramatic events of a folktale are a little easier to handle. Animals help us follow the story with a little bit of distance to it, that is, they impart enough psychological distance to keep a frightening story from being truly terrifying. Sometimes we need the disguise or symbolism of animals to talk about what is important. Animals are neuter. They aren't specific, like crazy Aunt Gertrude or cruel Uncle Horatio. Animals can represent us in fur, feather, or fin, but as characters they make the story medicine a little easier to take. Stories are rehearsals for the future, and as such animals make this easier.

Animals can also be symbols: the sly fox, the clever wolf, or the powerful bear. In fact, we often describe people with references to animals, such as: gentle as a dove, cheerful as a lark, timid as a rabbit, fierce as a tiger, brave as a lion, proud as a peacock, innocent as a lamb, faithful as a dog, henpecked, birdlike, a lone wolf, a real hog, and stubborn as a mule.

Sometimes it is beneficial for children to see a helpless animal such as a rabbit outsmart an animal that is big and strong. After all, aren't children relatively helpless in the world of adults? Wouldn't it be easy for them to unconsciously relate to Br'er Rabbit as he outwits the other animals? Doesn't that give readers and listeners a sense of power, an "I can do it too" spirit?

The fables have colored our attitudes toward moral and ethical problems. They are part of our everyday life and speech. Fables are brief narratives that take abstract ideas of good or bad, wise or foolish behavior and attempt to make them concrete and striking enough to be understood and remembered. The characters are usually beasts that behave like human beings and have one dominant trait. They remain coldly impersonal and engage in a single significant act that teaches a moral lesson.

Fables praise not the heroic virtues, but rather the peasant virtues of discretion, prudence, moderation, and forethought. They are pieces of literature found in any culture story collection that the ordinary people can identify with. Fables slipped in among warmly appealing folktales and modern realistic stories provide abstractions to consider, and are pithy maxims passed down to us by our wise predecessors throughout the ages.

Archetypal needs are basic human needs or requirements—love, security, understanding, acceptance, success, community and companionship, happiness, and knowledge. Archetypal story features recall truths embedded deep in memory. This is a tool that can be used to expand and extend human knowing and human awareness. Through the use of archetypes, we find ourselves within the story. We become the story, in a sense, and its truth lives in us.

Today, perhaps more than ever, we need to see ourselves in story, through which we can transcend human differences and technological changes and understand our culture, religion, and language. This is our inheritance. It binds us together in recognition of our universal commonalities at a rich level of humanness. As W. R. S. Ralston (1873) expressed it, "One touch of storytelling may, in some instances, make the whole world kin."

In traditional Navajo belief, a person's worth is determined by the stories and songs she or he knows, because it is by this knowledge that an individual is linked to the history of the entire group. Author Isak Dinesen said, "All sorrows can be borne if you put them into a story or tell a story about them." Joseph Campbell stated, "Fairytales represent psychological, not physical triumphs."

We know the same stories, and when we retell them, we do more than keep departed people alive; we keep ourselves alive as well. The Japanese claim that a person is not dead until people stop using his name.

With stories we can focus on our commonalities along with our differences. The high school cliques of today feed upon discrimination, encouraging bullies and ridiculing others. There is always the wish that these behaviors can be addressed in a meaningful way. They can be—through stories! Starting at the beginning and continuing throughout our children's lives, stories can help serve as vaccination against social pressures.

If we want our youngsters to grow up with tolerance, we must recognize one another's differences and not only accept them, but also celebrate them. This requires respect and understanding. May the following stories help nurture humanity and compassion, linking adults and children everywhere.

ABOUT THIS BOOK

This book is a collection of stories that demonstrate and impart profound truths about character and values. Some of the stories are ancient, predating written history, and some are more recent. They come from diverse cultures and regions that span the continents. There are stories from Zen Buddhists in Asia, from Paiute Indians of North America, and from the Maoris of New Zealand. Some are folktales, some are fables, and others are sacred literature or true stories from history.

The tales are arranged in broad categories under specific themes of character traits, values, and related issues. These categories are intentionally broad because the specific terminology for values is continually evolving, and because for each user, the needs may be different. It is important to keep in mind that a story in the section on perseverance, for example, may be equally appropriate and applicable to studies on patience, or, with some creativity, even to additional themes.

Who is this book intended for? Like folktales throughout history, this collection of stories is for people of all ages. It is made up of the tales that have lasted to today in the efforts of people to teach and provide examples of behavior—behavior that develops good community people and strong citizens.

Teachers who are beginning a unit on a particular value or character trait may want to introduce the lesson with one of these stories, then use the activity ideas to help enhance the lesson. Librarians will find this collection useful for story hours and may also want to add it to the teacher bookshelf. They can also recommend it to students who are researching character education issues.

Parents may reach for this collection when a specific issue comes up with a child—these stories are great launches for family discussions.

Activities and discussion questions provided with the stories are meant to help educators and parents extend learning through a variety of ways and varied use of the senses. This is not material for preaching, but instead provided so individuals can make their own connections—connections that they recognize and appreciate.

Students, parents, teachers, librarians, and all professionals who are looking for solutions to some of our modern problems will find answers in these stories of old. Times may change, but people, their needs, and problems remain the same.

A *final word:* the author encourages a sharing of these stories through storytelling, just as they have been passed down to us, as well as by reading the text. Try it, you'll like it!

Love

The Bamboo Princess
(Japan)

Once upon a time in Japan, a gentle old couple lived deep in a bamboo forest. The couple was lonely because they were childless and had always wanted a family of their own to love and care for. This old couple was quite poor. The old man earned money by cutting bamboo and selling the pieces that his wife made into baskets, tableware, hats, and other things. As so often is the case, the man was referred to by his occupation, Bamboo-cutter, and his wife was called Weaver of Bamboo.

Bamboo-cutter was at work one dreary day deep in a dark bamboo thicket. He was carefully selecting straight bamboo to cut because his wife had requested some that would be easy to work with. Deep in the thicket, Bamboo-cutter noticed something that was unlike anything he had ever seen before. There seemed to be one slender bamboo plant that had a golden glow. After carefully examining the special bamboo, he cut it open to see if he could discover what was causing its eerie glow.

What he found inside the hollow bamboo stem was amazing! There was a perfect tiny baby girl who was about three inches high. Bamboo-cutter held her gently in the palm of one of his callused hands. He hurried home to Weaver of Bamboo as carefully as he could. When he arrived and opened the door, he called out, "Weaver of Bamboo, come see what I have found. Come see this special gift. We have at last our very own daughter!"

Weaver of Bamboo looked into his hand and saw the tiny golden girl. "Isn't she the most beautiful thing you have ever seen?" she gasped. Bamboo-cutter told her all about how he had seen the eerie bamboo stalk, cut it carefully, opened it, and found this tiny person. After discussing what they should name this miracle child, the couple finally decided to call her Bamboo Princess.

As if having Bamboo Princess wasn't unique enough, from that day on, Bamboo-cutter came upon bamboo that had the same eerie glow. When he cut these stalks, though, he found piles of gold coins inside each of them. Before long, the old couple was very wealthy indeed and able to provide luxuries for their Bamboo Princess.

Bamboo Princess grew as much as an inch each day, not only bigger, but also lovelier. She seemed to radiate joy and filled their lives with great happiness. Bamboo-cutter enjoyed nothing more than watching Bamboo Princess chase dragonflies as they flew from flower to flower. His heart was filled with joy. "Little Bamboo Princess," he told her one day as he held her in his arms, "there is nothing in this world that I wouldn't do for you. You are my special joy."

As she grew each day, Bamboo Princess soon became a beautiful young maiden. Mere mortal young men who chanced to see her of course fell hopelessly in love. Word spread about this beauty, and young noblemen were soon courting her and begging for her hand in marriage.

"I shall never marry," Bamboo Princess would tell one and all. "Dear mother and father, I will never leave your side." Of course, Bamboo-cutter was pleased to hear her say this because he never wanted her to leave them alone and lonely again. There were five suitors of great wealth and noble bearing that stood out from the others and were persistent. They were outside her home every day, begging for a chance to visit with her.

Bamboo-cutter tried to discourage these five young men, but in time he began to feel sorry for them. If he were young again and saw Bamboo Princess, he too would be most earnest in wooing her. Taking pity on them, he decided to ask Bamboo Princess to choose one of them for a husband. "I have thought about it," he told her, "and decided that you should marry the one who is able to bring you a golden bough laden with fruit of living amber, an animal skin with fur of purest gold, a necklace made of dragons' eyes, paper that lights up the darkness, and a fan that shines like the rising sun."

When Bamboo-cutter told the five suitors what tasks they were to perform, the young men set off immediately, promising to return with the gifts. Of course, these tasks were easier said than done. "Maybe, Weaver of Bamboo, these will be impossible things for them to obtain and they will give up their dreams of marrying our Bamboo Princess," he told his wife.

Months later, to Bamboo-cutter's great surprise, all five young men returned with the fabulous treasures. Each of them held out marvels of the amber fruit, the golden fur, the shining fan, the dragons'-eye necklace, and the luminous paper as they bowed quite low to Bamboo Princess. But her natural beauty outshone the glittering baubles, and the five guilty men were forced to admit that their marvels were fakes. The young noblemen left heartbroken and never gazed upon their beloved princess again.

The old couple was secretly pleased that their daughter would not marry and move away, leaving them to be lonely again. But such peace didn't last long because in the eighth month of that year, Bamboo Princess would sit each night and stare at the moon waxing fuller in the sky. As the moon grew brighter, Bamboo Princess's eyes grew more wistful and melancholy. "What makes you look so sad, daughter?" Weaver of Bamboo asked.

Bamboo Princess looked at her old mother and burst into tears. "Oh, dear mother, I wish I could stay with you forever," she cried. "Soon I must return though."

"Return?" asked Bamboo-cutter. "Return where?"

She looked at him and, with tears in her eyes, replied, "to the city of the moon where I was born."

Her mother and father asked in unison, "The city of the moon?"

"Yes," she answered. "Now that I am grown, they will be coming for me."

"Who will be coming for you?" Bamboo-cutter asked.

"When will they be coming for you?" implored her mother.

"On the fifteenth night of this month, when the moon is full, the moon people will come for me," was her quiet answer.

"Oh no!" screamed the old mother. "That is tomorrow! I won't allow it!"

Bamboo-cutter added, "You are our daughter. No one can take you from us!" The old couple embraced her and wept. "Mark our words, Bamboo Princess, we will never let you leave us," they sobbed.

Bamboo-cutter decided to make sure no one would come and take his daughter away. The very next day he hired more than a thousand strong samurai to protect her. They stood shoulder to shoulder and made a circle around the house. They even formed a column on the roof. When the moon began to rise over the mountains that evening, the samurai lifted their bows and pointed their arrows at the sky. Inside the house, Bamboo-cutter, Weaver of Bamboo, and Bamboo Princess sat together.

The full moon rose and cast a glow of light upon the samurai, who let their arrows fly toward the moon. The arrows vanished in the sky and the moonbeams pierced the warriors' armor. Each and every warrior stood paralyzed.

Two moon maidens with a winged horse and chariot appeared from out of the unearthly light of the moon. At the same time, Bamboo Princess silently walked outside, as if under a spell. The old couple knew that there was nothing they could do to keep her from leaving them. They ran out of the house after her and cried, "If you must go, take us with you."

"Oh how I wish I could. You have no idea how much I will miss you. As a token of my gratitude for the care and love you have showed me, take this as a reminder." As she said this, she dropped a pouch to the ground. "Take this medicine. It will keep you from growing older. You will never grow older. May you always be healthy and happy and remember me. Goodbye!"

With this, Bamboo Princess stepped into the waiting silver chariot and the winged horse leaped upward to the sky. The old couple watched the horse and chariot and the heavenly maidens fade away to the light of the moon.

Later that night, they built a small fire outside and sat beside it. The old man was holding the magic pouch that Bamboo Princess had given them. "With this medicine we can live forever," they sighed. They looked up at the bright full moon and said, "But without you, our wonderful Bamboo Princess, we can never be happy again. What good would our lives be without such happiness?" Their eyes met and with these words, Bamboo-cutter tossed the pouch into the fire where the flames caught it and spewed forth sparks and showers of light.

Lovers in the Sky
(China)

If you look to the heavens on the seventh night of the seventh month, you will see some very special stars. One of the stars is called Herding Boy Star and the other is called Weaving Girl Star.

Many turns of the earth ago, a silver river separated the heavens and the earth. In the celestial heavens lived a girl called Weaving Girl. She was the most beloved grandchild of the Queen Mother. Weaving Girl was not only lovely, but also very gentle. Her hands were slender, and she could weave the most beautiful cloth. She had six sisters who also could weave, and each day they would make different patterns of cloth. Sometimes they would weave a cloud for the heavens.

At this same time, on Earth, there lived a young orphan boy whose parents had died when he was very young. His name was Herding Boy and he lived with his older brother and his brother's wife. They were very poor.

One day, the elder brother decided to divide their property. Naturally, he kept everything for himself and gave Herding Boy only a very old ox. Herding Boy did not complain, and took very good care of his ox, bringing the animal to a lovely plain to eat grass and then to a watering hole. The ox somehow seemed to understand the boy's problems.

The ox worked diligently for his new master, tilling and plowing the earth. Soon after, the area where the ox had plowed became extremely fertile ground so that anything Herding Boy planted grew abundantly. With the money that the boy saved from selling the crops, he bought a house and built a large corral for his ox.

Even though Herding Boy was happy, he was lonely because he had no one to talk with. One day, he remarked to the ox, "I wish I had a companion." To Herding Boy's surprise, the ox answered, "That's not such a difficult task." The ox continued, "There are seven fairies now swimming in the river. Their clothes are on the banks of the river. If you quickly go to the river unseen and gather up the clothes of one of the fairies, she will have to remain and be your wife. Quickly now, get on my back and I will take you to the river."

It was just as the ox had said. There in the river, seven beautiful fairies were playing. It was Weaving Girl and her six sisters having a bath. Seven garments, all of different colors, lay on the riverbank—red, green, blue, purple, pink, yellow, and white. Herding Boy decided to take the garment that was all white.

As he ran away, the fairies saw him and were frightened. They ran onto the shore and put their clothes on, but Weaving Girl could not find hers. She started sobbing and begged the young man to return her clothes. Herding Boy answered, "Only if you will be my wife will I return your clothes." There was nothing Weaving Girl could do but nod "yes." After receiving her clothes and putting them on, she returned with Herding Boy to his home and became his wife.

Ten years passed and the couple now had two beautiful children: a girl, age five; and a boy, age six. The ox had been very old when Herding Boy received it, and by now it was about to die. The ox said to Herding Boy, "When I die, skin my hide and put the hide on whenever you have any troubles." With that, the animal died. The couple mourned the ox and was filled with grief. Herding Boy skinned the hide of the ox just as he had been told to do.

In heaven, ten years was like only ten days. Since Weaving Girl had disappeared, no more clouds were woven. The Queen Mother was very upset and ordered, "Weaving Girl must be brought back to the heavens."

At that very moment on Earth, Weaving Girl was busy weaving some very beautiful cloth. Her children were at her side when suddenly it became very dark, lightning flashed across the sky, and the thunder was horrendous. The children started to cry, when a magpie flew down from the heavens. "You must return to the heavens," said the magpie. "The Queen Mother says you must come back."

Weaving Girl's face turned white and she blurted, "I will not return. I will not return."

"If you do not return, your whole family here on Earth will be punished," cautioned the magpie.

As the thunder continued to boom, heavenly soldiers came down to Earth and started to take Weaving Girl to heaven. Her children sobbed, "Don't take our mother away." At the same time, Herding Boy chased the heavenly soldiers, shouting, "Return my wife!" He put his children in a basket and carried them with him. He ran hard and fast and chased the soldiers to the silver river.

The Queen Mother, seeing that Herding Boy was close to her soldiers, quickly removed the silver river and threw it into the sky. With this act, he could no longer give chase. Suddenly, Herding Boy remembered the hide of the ox. When he threw it onto his back, he was able to run into the heavens. He was almost near the silver river, now in the sky, when the Queen Mother tossed a golden hairpin into the river. At once the river became very wide, so wide, in fact, that Herding Boy could not get across it. The expression on his face was filled with despair. Weaving Girl tried to express her love for him. They both showed their anguish about being kept apart.

Seeing all of this, the Queen Mother was deeply moved. She then agreed that once a year on the seventh day of the seventh month, the two could cross the silver river and meet again. She asked the magpies to stretch their wings to make a bridge on that day so the couple could meet.

Now, when you look into the sky on the seventh day of the seventh month, you will see a very bright star and two little stars. These are Herding Boy and his two children. The other star, separated by the Milky Way, is Weaving Girl. At a certain time of the night, the Milky Way, which is the silver river, will appear. Then in an instant, you will see the star of Herding Boy and the star of Weaving Girl meet, only to be separated again by daylight.

Today, children often make seven flowers, chairs, and dresses in miniature for the seven fairies. It is considered a time when young girls pray for the right husband-to-be. Everyone looks into the sky trying to find the stars of Herding Boy and Weaving Girl. Do you think you can find them in the night sky?

Note: This story is a variation on the legend of the Blue Willow dinnerware pattern.

The Lovers of Spirit Lake
(Native American, Iowa, USA)

In ancient times, the native people of Iowa captured a beautiful maiden. They took her to a grove of trees by Spirit Lake and made preparations to sacrifice her to the spirits of the sky. This maiden was so beautiful and gentle that one of the young braves fell in love with her. When he saw her soft, sad brown eyes, he knew he must do something. He loved her too much to see her die and was determined to save her.

He took two horses to a small valley on the opposite side of the lake and tied them loosely to some bushes. Then, carefully hiding his canoe in a place near the grove where the prisoner was kept, he waited. Finding an opportunity to set her free, he took the maiden's hand and hurried her to his canoe. They quietly got in and he began to paddle across the lake. When they had made it to the middle of the lake, suddenly a strong wind boiled from the clouds across the water. Waves swamped the canoe and it sank. Both the maiden and her lover were drowned.

The spirits of the water took pity on the couple. They escorted the lovers to a shining cave under the lake and gave it to them for their very own.

There they dwell to this very day in peace and happiness.

The Parable of the Good Samaritan
(New Testament, Christian Bible
Luke 10:30–35)

A man was attacked and beaten by robbers. He was lying on the side of the road where his attackers had left him for dead. People passed by him without stopping, including a priest and a Levite. A Samaritan fellow who was traveling by, stopped and was filled with sorrow and kindness for this man—this man he had never even seen before.

With that, the Samaritan bandaged the man's wounds and took him to a nearby village. The Samaritan even paid for the man to stay in a hotel until he was healed and able to go about on his own again.

The Selkie
(Scotland)

Long ago and at a foggy place where people rarely got a chance to read the stars in the sky, there was a fisherman from the McCodrum clan who fished regularly off the waters of the Hebridean Islands. The Outer Hebrides were windswept, with rugged cliffs, clean beaches, tiny bays, and many archaeological treasures from the seas and invaders.

The hardworking fisherman happened upon some other treasures of the seas. He discovered seven naked girls dancing on the shore. They leaped, spun, and enjoyed the freedom of the beach, floating in the air as they danced with joy. On a large boulder which lay further down the beach were seven sealskins. He had heard stories of the selkies, who were seals of the sea but became human girls when they were on the land and had shed their sealskins.

"These girls must be selkies!" he thought. "I'll creep up on the skins and steal one of them." He knew, again from the stories, that if one of the girls could not resume her seal shape inside her sealskin, she would be forced to stay in human form.

"Aha!" he said, as he snatched the most beautiful of the skins from the boulder.

When the dancing maidens heard this and saw him with the skin, they all rushed to the boulder to get their skin and escape. Of course, now one of them was doomed to be human.

"You have no other choice but to become my wife," the fisherman told her.

"Please kind sir," she begged, "give me my skin and allow me to return to the sea where I belong."

"No," he said firmly. "You must stay in your present form and become my wife."

They argued, she pleaded, and he insisted. And so it was. They married and had two children, Fiona and Sava. He hid her sealskin where he felt certain she would never find it. He grew to love her and was gentle and considerate while she learned to care for him, but she had a haunted look in her eyes that never left.

So, they aged together. One day, the old fisherman left home to fish in the fog. While he was gone, his wife searched all through their home. She came across an old chest hidden upstairs in a locked back room. She opened it with a heart that was beating like a person who had just finished running a long distance and climbing high mountains. Inside the chest was her sealskin.

She waited until her husband came home with a respectable catch of fish. They ate supper and he yawned, stretched, and he and his wife went to bed. In the middle of the night, she crept away and ran down to the beach, wrapped her sealskin around her, and returned at last to her own people in the sea.

The selkie's husband found the opened chest and knew what had happened. Forlornly, he prowled the beaches calling to her, but he never saw his wife again.

The Scottish clan of the seal woman was known afterward as McCodrum of the Seals. You can recognize their descendants because all of them have wee webs of skin between their fingers and toes.

Thoughts About the Stories, Discussions, and Activities

THE BAMBOO PRINCESS

This story is a variation on many others about the desire of a lonely old couple to have a child of their own to love. This variant is from Japan.

- ⊙ *Can you find additional stories with the theme of "The Bamboo Princess" from other countries? Check folktale collections in your library and make a list. Mark the stories and their country of origin on a map. What does this tell us about the story and its themes?*
- ⊙ *Visit a retirement home and interview childless couples there. Did they wish for children? Did they regret not becoming parents? If so, why? Use your findings to write a different version of this folktale, with love as a theme.*
- ⊙ *What are some options available for becoming parents today? Why do you think people want to have children so much?*
- ⊙ *Interview adoptive parents to find out why they made their decision and to get their thoughts on adoption in general. Then write an essay on love and adoption.*

LOVERS IN THE SKY

This story is similar to "Romeo and Juliet," since it concerns lovers who are separated by others.

- ⊙ *Do you personally know any young people who are forbidden to see each other? What would you feel, think, or do in a similar situation? Discuss your ideas with others.*
- ⊙ *Read the story of "Romeo and Juliet," then make a list of the similarities and differences between these two stories. What do they tell us about love? Is the message the same?*

THE LOVERS OF SPIRIT LAKE

This is a tale of love that endures beyond life.

- ⊙ *Reread the story. What is its theme? Can you find any other folktales that involve this theme? Research folktale collections in the library and make a list to share with others.*
- ⊙ *Many stories and legends contain symbols. What are the symbols in this story?*

THE GOOD SAMARITAN

This story from the Christian Bible is a parable of kindness and love toward others.

- ⊙ *Investigate sacred books from other religions and cultures to discover if there are any stories similar to "The Good Samaritan." You can probably find these in your local library. How are the stories similar? How are they different? Share your discoveries.*

THE SELKIE

This is a familiar story of love and transformation.

- ⊙ *What is a transformation and how is it related to love? Discuss this, drawing upon your own experiences.*
- ⊙ *Search out other stories of transformation and compare and contrast them.*

Other Activity Ideas

- *One way to share love with both the people you know and those you don't is by performing random acts of kindness. This is not just a slogan, but is actually a Denver-based foundation that uses its $5 million annual budget to promote kindness. It has offshoots in 135 countries. People always remember the acts of kindness someone does for them. There is power in that. Here are some examples of the idea:*

  - *A twelve-year-old girl in Idaho asked friends to celebrate her birthday at an animal shelter and told them all to bring beds, toys, and leashes for the animals.*
  - *A Fargo, North Dakota, flower shop gave a dozen roses each to hundreds of passersby, asking that the recipients give a rose to everyone they met.*
  - *In Overland Park, Kansas, a woman hospital chaplain organized massage therapists to give free massages to staff members at three local hospitals. Six hundred people got the massages.*
  - *In Lacey, Washington, the town's senior citizens group called Random Acts, fixed sixty Thanksgiving meals and served them to disabled seniors.*

Here are some random acts of kindness that you might try:

- *Buy a pizza for a neighbor family.*

- *Clean up trash, rake an elderly neighbor's leaves, pull weeds, shovel snow, donate old clothes, open a door, and give a hug or a compliment.*
- *Keep a log of the number of kind acts you do in a week. Keep a similar list of your unkind acts also.*
- *Plan some future kind action and track the results discovered.*
- *Give apples to people who are on their way to work. Or smile, wave, and say "hello" to people on the street.*
- *Hand out balloons to strangers.*
- *Give your old toys to children at a safe house.*
- *Pay for the meal of the person behind you in a drive-through line.*
- *Bake cookies and take them to fire and police stations.*
- *Search your school or public library for the book entitled* Random Acts, *published in 1993 by Donari Press in Berkeley, California. This is a collection of stories of people who had received or committed random acts of kindness. Which story inspires you the most? Are there ideas you could use in your own life? What are they?*
- *Read and discuss Martin Goldsmith's book,* The Inextinguishable Symphony *(Wiley & Sons), a true story of music and love in Nazi Germany. Use the library or Internet to research other historical acts of kindness during World War II, World War I, or the American Civil War and write a report on one of them.*
- *In families, there are many ways to show love. These include:*

  - *When there is conflict in your family, meet in a neutral but cozy place for discussions. Find out how the conflict began, because many times people don't remember. Rephrase the conflict to have it make more sense.*
  - *Share happy memories of better times. Photograph albums are a good source for remembering.*
  - *Look toward the future and plan something together, because time is running short for all of us and we need to spend more time in positive ways.*

See the "General Activities" section at the back of this book for more ideas to further explore these topics.

Appreciation

The Delicious Strawberry
(Zen Buddhist)

One blessed day in an Asian jungle, a happy young man strolled along a monkey path, playing a love tune on his mouth harp. As he played, he thought of the maiden of his devotions, and looked forward to playing his music for her alone.

With his attention focused on future joy, he never heard the soft padded footsteps behind him until they were quite close. He turned his head to see who was there, and before his eyes was a tiger crouched down in a stalking stance. Drool was coming from the tiger's mouth as he eyed his next meal—the young musician!

Instinctively, the young man turned away from the tiger and started to dash through the jungle on the monkey path. He heard the plomph! plomph! of the tiger's feet behind him. Suddenly, the path ended at an abrupt cliff that was covered with trees and vines on which the monkeys probably traveled. Far below, he saw rocks and another tiger pacing and looking up the cliffside. But the tiger behind him was only one leap away, so the young man jumped off the cliff and started to fall.

On his way down, he grasped for a bush that he saw growing out of the mountain. He caught it and swung in the air, but the roots of the bush were deep. There he was—hanging between two frustrated and hungry tigers. His eyes went to the bush and branches he was clinging to. There, before his startled eyes was a small strawberry bush with a single ripe glistening strawberry.

He carefully removed one of his hands from the branch he clutched, reached out for the strawberry, plucked it, and slowly put it in his mouth. Ah, it was the most delicious strawberry he had tasted in all of his life.

The Stonecutter
(Japan)

Long ago, in ancient times, the fury of fire erupted from deep in the oceans and blew up to the surface where the molten lava of the volcanoes spewed forth, cooled, and formed the islands of Japan. People who came to this land of mountains and oceans needed tools and material to build with. And so each day the Stonecutter took his place on the mountain, and with hammer and chisel cut the stone to provide building blocks and smaller pieces for arrows, spears, blades, and scraping tools.

Every day the Stonecutter rejoiced in the sounds of his labor, the hammer of steel on rock. Then one day, he heard a most captivating sound from down by the road. It was the music of many musicians playing in a procession of guards, happy people, and various entertainers in which a rich man of royalty was being carried. Not only were the sounds of the music exciting to the ear, but there was also beauty all around, with rich clothing, banners, and the bright sparkling and shining swords and shields carried by the guards. Colored lights reflected everywhere, and the gently flapping banners brought joy to the eyes.

The Stonecutter sat back on his haunches and looked at his mountain. "Oh Spirit of the mountain. I would wish to be as wealthy and powerful as this man of royalty." His envy shone in his eyes. Before the Stonecutter knew what was happening, the mountain Spirit transformed him into a respected man of royalty. Servants obeyed his every demand and he felt the power of his position. Everyone paid him respect and granted him his every wish.

No longer did the Stonecutter live in a humble hut; he dwelled in a mighty palace full of riches and surrounded by well-tended gardens. All sorts of fragrant blossoms bloomed there. One day, as he was walking in his gardens smelling the delicate flowers, the hot sun beating down on the earth caught his attention. The scorching sun burned the delicate plants and caused them to wilt and droop.

The Stonecutter again called upon the mountain Spirit and asked for the power of the sun. "The sun has so much power. It can change growing things at will. I would have that power." As before, the mountain Spirit answered his wishes and changed him into the sun. With his new power, the Stonecutter brought all of his heat and brightness down on the earth. Plants withered and died, the refreshing streams of water dried up, and the land became cracked and parched. The Stonecutter could see his new power everywhere he went.

Then, a dark cloud that drifted overhead blotted out the sun's rays. Again, the Stonecutter was struck by the power of the clouds over the sun. "Oh mountain Spirit, I would be the clouds. They have great power over the sun," he implored. And again, it was so. The Stonecutter was transformed into banks of roiling clouds. "Look at my power now," he roared as he stirred up gigantic storms. Thunder and lightning crashed out of his clouds. Rains came down in torrents, flooding the land and washing away every structure. The Stonecutter wreaked havoc with his new power.

There was nothing that could withstand the powers of the storms...except...the mountain. The immense mountain stood in the middle of the floods—strong, powerful, and unmovable.

Seeing this, the Stonecutter made one more request of the mountain Spirit. "Make me become a mountain!" he demanded. Now he stood, secure that he was the ultimate power. Then he felt something deep within him—the ringing sound of a lowly stonecutter's hammer and chisel. At last, the Stonecutter realized that everything has power and everything is also powerless. There is nothing on earth that is insignificant.

The Wind and the Sun
(Aesop)

An argument arose between the wind and the sun. "I am the stronger of the two of us," roared the wind.

"Ah, no indeed. I am the stronger!" said the sun.

"There is a traveler," said the wind. "Let us put it to the test by seeing which of us can get the man's coat off of him the soonest," he challenged.

"Fair contest," agreed the sun.

The wind went first and began sending ferocious blasts of air that threatened to blow the man off his feet. The wind blew and blew until there was no more air left to blow, but the man just bunched the coat up in front of him and hung on.

The sun told the wind, "Let me show you how to do it." The sun cleared the sky of all clouds and began to beam its most intense blazing heat. Shortly, the man was sweating and seemed about to pass out. He quickly flung off his coat and ran to find the nearest shady place.

"Do you now appreciate which of us is the stronger?" questioned the sun.

The Town Mouse
and the Country Mouse
(Aesop)

A fine gray country mouse with a long tail that was curly at its end invited his friend from the town to come visit him in the fields. On his arrival, the town mouse was disappointed to find that dinner consisted of common barleycorns and some earthy-tasting roots. "Dear friend," he commented, "you live here munching on things like an ant. You must come and visit me and I will show you gastronomic delights."

So, the town mouse took the country mouse back to the town with him. With his tail swishing back and forth, the town mouse introduced his friend to cheese, honey, figs, dates, and peanut butter. Of course, the country mouse was amazed. They hunkered down and ate until their stomachs were filled tight.

Then it happened. The door opened and someone came in. The two mice scurried off in alarm and squeezed themselves into an uncomfortable hole. When all seemed quiet, they wiggled out of the hole, but were forced to scuttle away again when another person came into the room.

By now, the country mouse was uncomfortably stuffed, alarmed, and scared. He had seen enough of the town to suit him. "I'm off. I can see that you live with delicious delights but there is too much danger along with it for my taste."

"Where are you going?" asked the town mouse as the country mouse started off.

"I am going home to the country. There I can enjoy my very simple meals in contented peace and comfort," was the answer.

Thoughts About the Stories, Discussions, and Activities

THE DELICIOUS STRAWBERRY

This story puts an everyday pleasure into extreme conditions, which enhances our appreciation.

⊙ *Have you ever experienced a time when something ordinary became something special to you? What do you think changed your thinking? Share these times.*

THE STONECUTTER

This is the classic story of a man unhappy with his role in life and a series of transformations that are just as unsatisfying.

⊙ *Reread the story and ponder the following themes. Then write an essay on one of them:*
  ⊙ *An individual can make a difference.*
  ⊙ *Always be yourself.*
  ⊙ *Obsession with greed and power leads to destruction.*
  ⊙ *Be careful what you wish for.*

⊙ *Notice the story's circular pattern, and consider its message that nothing is insignificant. How can this message be applied to contemporary society?*

THE WIND AND THE SUN

This fable inspires us to appreciate the power we have and use it in a positive fashion.

⊙ *In this story, the wind and sun are used as symbols of different types of power. What are they?*

⊙ *Research other symbols at your school or public library, including cultural examples, such as the prominent role of freedom and transcendence symbols in Celtic myth and legend. These include birds as symbols of liberation from earthly ties, able to soar in spiritual communication with the heavens. Returning to earth, they bring messages of prophecy and guidance, aiding mortals on their spiritual and earthly journeys. What other cultures have similar symbols?*

THE TOWN MOUSE AND THE COUNTRY MOUSE

Here is another look at appreciating who we are, what we have, and where we are comfortable.

⊙ *Advertising in the media often gives us messages of who we should be and what we should have and appreciate. What are some of those messages? Can you think of any product advertisements that you do not appreciate?*

⊙ *Make a list of simple things in your life that you enjoy (e.g., walking in the rain without an umbrella, eating gooey pizza, rolling on the grass with your dog).*

⊙ *Do you have a friend who likes different things than you? Write an essay on your differences.*

Other Activity Ideas

- Writing in a journal is an activity a person appreciates months or years later. It is also a place to record the experiences and things you treasure. Start a journal listing your daily activities. Keep a log of books you read, movies you see, restaurants or places you visit. Try to list three things every day that you appreciate or are thankful for.

- Make a list of things you enjoyed five, ten, or fifteen years ago. What do you think you'll appreciate ten, twenty, or thirty years from now?

- Go to the library and discover oral history projects that capture the essence of localities and people. What do these materials tell you about a place, the people, and the times? Visit informally with older residents over coffee or tea to collect their memories and stories. This can help pass on knowledge from one generation to another before being lost forever. A lead-in question might be, "What do you have or know that we could write about?" Another question might be, "What are the events in your life that gave you the deepest appreciation?" or "What tidbits do you know that make this place come alive?" Share the results in a library, museum, school, or community center.

- Look up the word "appreciate" in the dictionary. How many meanings does it have, and how are these meanings related?

- Music gives us inspiration and helps us see that we are not alone or unusual. Some examples include gospel, jazz, and pop music. There are also messages in music about materialism versus appreciation (e.g., the Beatles, "Can't Buy Me Love"). Think about the music you most appreciate, its themes, and how you feel when you listen to it. Jazz musician Wynton Marsalis says, "The feeling of jazz is like the feeling you get going into your favorite grandmother's house. The feeling there is warm." What music gives you that feeling?

⊙ Following September 11, 2001, patriotic music helped people share an appreciation for our country. Share music that inspires you, music that you can relate to, or music that helps you.

⊙ Fine-tune your senses. Observe the beauty of nature, art, and the world around you using your sight, hearing, touch, smell, and taste. Write about your experience.

⊙ Poetry can aid appreciation. Consider the quote of Percy Bysshe Shelley (1792–1822): "Poetry is the record of the best and happiest moments of the happiest and best minds." Write a poem about your happiest moments.

⊙ The Roman poet Horace (65 B.C.O.–8 B.C.) said, "Drop the question what tomorrow may bring and count as profit every day that Fate allows you." What does this mean to you? Discuss.

⊙ Sir James Barrie (Scottish author of Peter Pan, 1860–1937) summed up work, play, and joy: "Nothing is really work unless you would rather be doing something else." What does this quote have to contribute to your appreciation of what you do?

See the "General Activities" section at the back of this book for more ideas to further explore these topics.

Perseverance

Robert the Bruce, the King
(Scotland)

Robert the Bruce (1271–1329) with skill and courage succeeded in freeing Scotland from England and, in defiance of the English, was crowned Robert I at Scone in 1306. His forces decisively defeated Edward II of England at the Battle of Bannockburn in 1314, demolishing the English armies. This was accomplished with an army of 6,000, which was outnumbered three to one by the English forces.

Other interesting facts about Robert the Bruce include Bruce's Well, which is behind St. Ninian's Episcopal Church in Prestwick. It is said that water from the well cured Robert the Bruce of leprosy from which he suffered for many years. It is also said that his heart is interred in the Melrose Abbey following his request that it be taken from his body and carried on crusade. Robert the Bruce had wanted to go on crusade, perhaps in expiation of the murder of John Comyn, and had received papal permission for the mutilation of his body necessary to remove his heart.

> Sir Robert the Bruce at Bannockburn
> Beat the English in every wheel and turn,
> And made them fly in great dismay
> From off the field without delay.
> 　　　　(William McGonagal, "The Battle of Bannockburn")

One of King Robert the Bruce's most notable attributes was that he never gave up. In his battles to free Scotland from England, his forces had lost numerous times, but still he persisted. The following incident is said to have taken place before the victory at Bannockburn.

One night after a battle was lost, Robert the Bruce was lying on a rude couch in his tent on the battlefield, quite despondent. His heart was heavy with the memory of his lost men and battles, and of the suffering throughout his country. Just then, he saw an industrious little spider in the corner of the tent, trying to fix its web to the top pole. It had already made six futile attempts; each time it tried, it fell.

Robert the Bruce recalled that he himself had lost six battles. Six! Both he and the spider had failed six times. And now he, King Bruce, was about to give up! Would the spider also be defeated in its attempts or would it persevere once again? At that moment, King Robert the Bruce made a promise to himself. If the small spider should try again to fix its web and be successful, then he too would profit by the spider's lesson and fight another battle.

Carefully, the spider made another attempt, slowly raising its shadowy body until, quivering in the air, it balanced itself for the final plunge. The king raised himself on his elbow and watched. In reality, a nation awaited that spider's success or failure! Again it plunged, caught at the pole, and triumphantly fixed its web. King Robert the Bruce jumped to his feet, threw his plaid about him, raised his clenched fist upwards to the sky, and began preparations for the greatest battle in Scottish history—the battle of Bannockburn. From that day forth, never again would the great king give up!

The Storyteller
(Ethiopia)

A hundred years ago, an African storyteller said that when one has traveled along a road he can sit down and wait for a story to overtake him. He also said that a story is like the wind. It comes from a far place and it can pass behind the back of a mountain. Here now is a tale about a clever farmer who outwitted a king in the land of Ethiopia.

There was a certain king who loved nothing so much as listening to stories. Every moment of his spare time was spent enjoying the tales told by the country's storytellers, but a day came when there were none left that he hadn't heard. His hunger for stories came to be known in the neighboring kingdoms, and wandering singers and storytellers came to the king to be rewarded for whatever new tales they could bring. But the more stories the king heard, the fewer were left that he had not. Finally, in desperation, he let it be known throughout the land that the storyteller who could make him cry, "Enough! No more!" would receive a great piece of land and the title of Ras, or prince.

Inspired by the thought of such wealth and honors, many men came to tell him stories, but he always sat and listened eagerly without ever protesting that he had heard too much. One day, a farmer came and offered to tell tales until the king was so full of them that he would cry out in protest. The king just smiled. "The best storytellers in Ethiopia have come and gone without telling me enough. And now, here you come in your simple innocence to win the land and the title of Ras," said the king. "Well, begin. You may at least try."

The humble farmer settled himself comfortably on a rug and began. "Once there was a peasant who sowed wheat. He mowed it when it was grown, threshed it, and put all the precious grain in his granary. It was a rich harvest, one of the best he had ever had. But this is the irony of the tale. In his granary there was a tiny flaw.

A hole big enough to pass a straw through. And when the grain was all stored, an ant came and went through the hole and found the wheat," the farmer continued. "He carried away a single grain of it to his anthill to eat."

"Aha!" exclaimed the king. "This is one of the stories that I have never heard. Continue."

So, the farmer continued, "The next day, another ant came and carried away a grain."

Once more the king exclaimed, "Aha!"

"The next day still another ant came and carried away a grain," said the storyteller with a gleam in his eye.

"Yes, yes, I understand," declared the king impatiently. "Let us get on with the story."

The storyteller nodded to the king. "The next day another ant came and carried away another grain. And the next day another ant came and carried away another grain."

The king interrupted, "Let us not dally with the details, the story is the thing."

"Indeed," said the farmer. "The next day another ant came."

"Please, please," demanded the king.

"But there are so many ants in this story," claimed the storyteller. "And the next day another ant came for a grain of wheat, and … "

The king frowned, "No, no, it must not be!"

"But there are so many ants in this story," continued the farmer. "And the next day another ant came for a grain of wheat, and … "

"No, no!" exploded the king. "It must not be!"

"Ah, but this is the crux of the story," said the farmer. "And the next day another ant came and took away a grain … "

The exasperated king interrupted the story, "But I understand all this. Let us pass over it and get on with the plot."

"Indeed," answered the storyteller. "And the next day another ant came and took his grain. And the next day … "

The king demanded, "Stop. I want no more of it!"

Modestly, the farmer explained, "The story must be told in the proper way. Besides, the granary is still nearly full of wheat and it must be emptied. That is the story. And the next day … "

"No, no, enough, enough!" roared the king.

But the farmer continued, "And the next day another ant … "

The king stood up and stamped his feet, "Enough, enough, you may have the land and the title of Ras!"

And so, the farmer storyteller became a prince and owned a great parcel of land. And this is what people mean when they say, "One grain at a time brings good fortune."

The Dragon and the Prince
(Poland)

There was an emperor who had three sons. One day the eldest son went out hunting. When he got outside the town, up sprang a hare out of a bush. The emperor's son went after it, hither and thither, until the hare fled into a watermill with the prince in pursuit. But the hare was really a dragon in disguise that waited for the prince and devoured him. After several days had elapsed and the prince did not return home, people began to wonder where he was.

Then the middle son went hunting. As he left the town, a hare sprang out of a bush and the prince chased it hither and thither into the watermill. But the hare was actually a dragon that waited for him and he also was devoured.

When some days had elapsed and neither prince returned, the whole court was in sorrow.

Then the third son went hunting to see if he could find his brothers. When he left town, again up sprang a hare out of a bush. The prince chased it hither and thither until the hare fled into the watermill. Instead of following it, this prince went on to find other game. "When I return I shall find you, hare," he said to himself.

The youngest prince went for a long time up and down the hill, but did not find anything. When he returned to the watermill, there was only an old woman there. The prince addressed her, "May good fortune help you old woman!"

The old woman answered him, "Good fortune to you my son!"

The prince asked the old woman, "Where, old woman, is the hare?"

She replied, "My son, that was not a hare, but a dragon. It kills and throttles many people."

The prince was somewhat disturbed when he heard this and said to the old woman, "What shall we do now? I fear that my two brothers probably perished here."

Her answer was, "They have indeed. There is not help for it. Go home my son, lest you follow them."

"Dear old woman, do you know what?" he said to her. "I know that you will be glad to liberate yourself from that pest."

The old woman interrupted him, "How should I not? It captured me too, in this way, but now I have no means of escape."

The prince continued, "Listen well to what I am going to say to you. Ask it whither it goes and where its strength is. Then kiss all that place where it tells you its strength is, as if from love. When you are certain about where that place is, tell me when I come to you."

The prince returned to the palace and the old woman remained in the watermill. When the dragon came in, the old woman began to question it, "Where have you been? Why do you go so far? You will never tell me where you go."

The dragon told her, "Well, my dear old woman, I do not go far."

Then the old woman began to coax it, "And why do you go? Tell me where your strength is. If I knew where your strength was, I don't know what I should do for love. I would kiss that place that gives you your strength."

The dragon smiled and said to her, "Yonder is my strength—in that fireplace." When the old woman began to pet and kiss the fireplace, the dragon burst into laughter. "Silly old woman, my strength isn't there. My strength is in that tree fungus in front of the house." The dragon laughed again as the old woman began to pet and kiss the tree. "Away old woman! My strength isn't there."

"Where is it?" demanded the old woman.

The dragon began to give an account of it in detail. "My strength is a long way off and you cannot go there. Far in another empire under the emperor's city is a lake. In that lake is a dragon. In that dragon is a boar. In that boar is a pigeon. In that pigeon is my strength."

The next morning, when the dragon went away from the mill, the prince came to the old woman and she told him all that she had heard from the dragon.

The prince disguised himself with shepherd's boots and staff and went into the world. After traveling from village to village and town to town, at last he came into another empire and into the imperial city where there was a lake under which the dragon sat. In town, the prince began to inquire who wanted a shepherd, and the citizens told him that the emperor did.

The prince went straight to the emperor. After he announced himself, the emperor admitted him into his presence and asked him, "Do you wish to keep sheep?"

"I do, illustrious one!" replied the prince.

Then the emperor engaged him and began to inform and instruct his new shepherd, "There is a lake here and alongside the lake is a very beautiful pasture. When you call the sheep out, they go thither at once and spread themselves around the lake. Whatever shepherd goes off there, that shepherd returns back no more. Therefore, my son, I tell you, don't let the sheep have their own way and go where they will. Keep them where you will."

The prince thanked the emperor and got himself ready. He called out the sheep and took with him two hounds that could catch a boar in the open country and a falcon that could capture any bird. This falcon also carried a pair of bagpipes. When he called out the sheep, he let them go at once to the lake, and they immediately spread around it. The prince placed the falcon on a stump, and the hounds and bagpipes underneath it, then tucked up his hose and sleeves and waded into the lake. He began to shout, "Dragon, dragon! Come out to single combat with me today that we may measure ourselves together, unless you are a weakling." This was, of course, intended as an insult.

The dragon called out in reply, "I will do so now prince—now!" Before long, the large, terrible dragon appeared. It was disgusting. The dragon seized the prince by the waist and they wrestled all afternoon. When the heat built up, the dragon said, "Let me go prince, that I may moisten my parched head in the lake and toss you to the sky."

The prince replied, "Come dragon. Don't talk nonsense. If I had the emperor's daughter to kiss me on the forehead, I would toss you still higher."

Thereupon the dragon suddenly let him go and went off into the lake. As evening approached, he washed and fixed himself up nicely. With the falcon on his arm and the hounds behind him, he put the bagpipes under his arm and then drove the sheep. He went into the town playing on the bagpipes.

When he returned to town, all of the citizens assembled to view his arrival as if it was a wondrous sight. No shepherd had ever returned from the lake. The next day, the prince got ready again and went with his sheep straight to the lake.

The emperor sent two grooms after him to go stealthily and see what he did. They placed themselves on a high hill where they could have a good view. When the prince arrived, he put the hounds and bagpipes under the stump and the falcon upon it. Then he tucked up his hose and sleeves and waded into the lake shouting, "Dragon, dragon! Come out to single combat with me that we may measure ourselves once more together unless you are a weakling!"

The dragon replied, "I will do so now prince, Now! Now!" The dragon appeared and it was large, terrible, and disgusting. It seized the prince by his waist and wrestled with him a summer's day until it was afternoon. When the afternoon heat came on, the dragon said, "Let me go prince, that I may moisten my parched head in the lake. I may toss you to the sky."

The prince replied, "Come dragon. Don't talk nonsense. If I had the emperor's daughter to kiss me on the forehead, I would toss you still higher."

Thereupon the dragon suddenly left hold of him and went off into the lake. When night approached, the prince drove the sheep as before and went home playing the bagpipes. When he arrived, the whole town was astir with wonder because the shepherd came home every evening. No one had been able to do that before.

The two grooms had already arrived at the palace before the prince and related everything they had heard and seen to the emperor. When the emperor saw that the shepherd returned home, he immediately summoned his daughter into his presence and told her everything. "But," said he, "tomorrow you must go with the shepherd to the lake and kiss him on the forehead." When the princess heard this, she burst into tears and began to beg her father, "You have no one but me. I am your only daughter. You don't care about me or care if I perish."

The emperor began to encourage and persuade her, "Don't fear, my daughter. You see that we have had so many changes of shepherds and all that went out to the lake, not a single one has returned. But this shepherd has been contending with the dragon for two whole days and it has not been able to hurt him. I assure you that he is able to overcome the dragon. Only go tomorrow with him to see whether he will free us from the mischief that has destroyed so many people."

The next day dawned and the sun came forth. The prince and the maiden both arose and began to prepare for going to the lake. The prince was cheerful; in fact, he was more cheerful than ever. The emperor's daughter was sad and shed tears, but the prince comforted her. "Dear princess, please do not weep. Do just as I tell you. When it is time, run up and kiss me and do not be afraid."

As he went and drove the sheep, the prince was thoroughly cheery. He played a merry tune on his bagpipes. The maiden did nothing but weep as she went beside him. Several times, he left off playing and turned toward her, "Weep not, golden one. Fear nought."

When they arrived at the lake, the sheep immediately spread around it and the prince placed the falcon on the stump. He placed the hounds and bagpipes under it and then tucked up his hose and sleeves and waded into the water. "Dragon," he shouted, "Dragon! Come out to single combat with me. Let us measure ourselves once more or are you a weakling?"

The dragon replied, "I will, prince. Now! Now!" Before long, the dragon appeared. It was huge. It was terrible. It was disgusting! When it came out, they seized each other by the middle and wrestled a summer's day until the afternoon. When the afternoon heat came on, the dragon said, "Let me go prince, that I may moisten my parched head in the lake and toss you to the skies."

The prince replied, "Come dragon! Don't talk nonsense. If I had the emperor's daughter to kiss me on the forehead, I would toss you much higher."

When he said this, the emperor's daughter ran up and kissed him on the face, on the eye, and on the forehead. Then he swung the dragon and tossed it high into the air. When it fell to the ground, it burst into pieces. Out of it sprang a wild boar that started to run away. The prince shouted to his shepherd dogs, "Hold it! Don't let it go!" The dogs sprang up, caught the boar, and soon tore it to pieces.

Out of the boar flew a pigeon. The prince then loosed the falcon, which caught the pigeon and brought it into the prince's hands. He said to it, "Tell me now! Where are my brothers?"

The pigeon replied, "I will tell you, only do me no harm. Immediately behind your father's town is a watermill. In the watermill are three wands that have sprouted up. Cut these three wands up from below and strike with them upon their root. An iron door will immediately open into a large vault. In that vault are many people. They are old and young, rich and poor, small and great, wives and maidens, so many people in fact that you could settle a populous empire with them. There, also, are your brothers."

As soon as the pigeon had told the prince all of this, he immediately wrung its neck.

The emperor had gone out in person and posted himself on the hill from which the grooms had viewed the shepherd. He too was a spectator of all that had taken place.

After the prince had thus obtained the dragon's head, twilight began to approach. He washed himself carefully and took the falcon on his shoulder. The hounds were behind him and the bagpipes were under his arm. He played them as he went, drove the sheep, and proceeded to the emperor's palace. The princess was still at his side and she was still in terror.

When they came to town, all of the villagers assembled as if to see a wonder. The emperor, who had seen all of the prince's heroism from the hill, called him into his presence and gave him the princess's hand. They went immediately to church and were married. The wedding festival continued for a week. After this, the prince told the emperor who he was and where he came from. The emperor and the whole town rejoiced still more upon hearing this. The prince was in a hurry to return to his own home, so the emperor gave him a large escort and equipped him for the journey.

When they were in the neighborhood of the watermill, the prince halted his escorts. He went inside, cut up the three wands, struck the root with them, and the iron door immediately opened. In the vault was a vast multitude of people. At the prince's order, they all came out one by one, until finally he saw his brothers. They all embraced and kissed.

After the whole multitude had emerged from the watermill, they thanked him for releasing and delivering them and they all left for their own homes. The three princes returned to their father's house. The youngest son and his wife lived a full happy reign until the end of their days.

The Singing, Soaring Lark
(Germany)

There once was a man who was about to set out on a long journey. On parting, he asked his three daughters what he should bring back for them. The eldest wished for pearls, the second for diamonds, but the third said, "Dear father, I should like a singing, soaring lark."

The father said, "Yes, if I can get it, you shall have it," kissed all three, and set out.

When the time came for him to return home again, he brought pearls and diamonds for the two eldest. He sought everywhere in vain for a singing, soaring lark for the youngest and he was very unhappy about it, for she was his favorite child. His road lay through a forest, in the midst of which was a splendid castle with a tree that stood nearby. Quite on the top of the tree, he saw a singing, soaring lark. "Aha, you come just at the right moment!" he said, quite delighted, and called to his servant to climb up and catch the little creature.

As the father approached the tree, a lion leapt from beneath it, shook himself, and roared till the leaves on the tree trembled. "He who tried to steal my singing, soaring lark," the lion cried, "will I devour."

Then the man said, "I did not know that the bird belonged to you. I will make amends for the wrong I have done and ransom myself with a large sum of money, only spare my life."

The lion snarled, "Nothing can save you unless you promise to give me for my own what first meets you on your return home.

If you will do that, I will grant you your life and you will have the bird for your daughter into the bargain."

The man hesitated. "That might be my youngest daughter, she loves me best, and always runs to meet me on my return home."

The servant, however, was terrified and said, "Why should your daughter be the very first to meet you? It might as easily be a cat or a dog." The man allowed himself to be persuaded. They took the singing, soaring lark, and promised to give the lion whatsoever should meet the father first on his return home.

When he entered his house, the first who met him was no other than his youngest and dearest daughter. She came running up, kissed and embraced him, and when she saw that he had brought her a singing, soaring lark, she was beside herself with joy.

The father, however, could not rejoice, but began to weep and said, "My dearest child, I have bought the little bird at a dear price. In return for it, I have been obliged to promise you to a savage lion. When he has you he will tear you in pieces and devour you." He told her what had happened and begged her not to go there, come what might.

She consoled him and said, "Dearest father, indeed your promise must be fulfilled. I will go forth and soften the lion, so that I may return to you safely."

The next morning she had the road pointed out to her, took leave, and went fearlessly into the forest. The lion, however, was actually an enchanted prince. He and his people were lions by day, but in the night, they resumed their natural human shapes. On the youngest daughter's arrival, she was kindly received and led into the castle. When night came, the lion turned into a handsome man and their wedding was celebrated with great magnificence. They lived happily together, remained awake at night, and slept in the daytime.

One day the prince came and said, "Tomorrow there is a feast in your father's house. Your eldest sister is going to be married. If you want to go there, my lions will accompany you."

She said, "Yes, I should like very much to see my family again," and so she went there along with the lions.

There was great joy when she arrived because they had all believed that she had been torn to pieces by the lion and had long been dead. She told them what a handsome husband she had and how well off she was. She remained with them while the wedding feast lasted and then went back to the forest.

When the second daughter was about to be married, and she was again invited to the wedding, she said to the prince, "This time I will not be alone. You must come with me."

"It would be too dangerous for me," he said. "If a ray from a burning candle falls upon me, I will be changed into a dove and for seven long years I would have to fly about with the doves."

"Ah, but do come with me. I will take great care of you and guard you from all light," she begged. So they went away together and took with them their little child as well. She had a room built there so strong and thick that no ray of light could pierce through it. There the lion prince was to shut himself in when the candles were lit for the wedding feast. However, the door to this room was made of green wood that had warped and left a little crack that no one noticed.

The wedding was celebrated with magnificence. When the procession with all of its candles and torches came back from church and passed by this apartment, a ray about the breadth of a hair fell on the prince and in-stantly transformed him. When the princess came in and looked for her husband, she saw only a white dove sitting there. The dove said to her, "For seven years I must fly about the world. At every seventh step that you take I will let fall a drop of red blood and a white feather. These will show you the way. If you follow the trace, you will be able to release me."

Thereupon, the dove flew out of the door and she followed him. At every seventh step, a red drop of blood and a little white feather fell down and showed her the way. She went continually further and further in the wide world, never looking about her or resting. When the seven years were almost past, she rejoiced and thought that they would soon be deliv-ered. Far from it! As they were moving onward, suddenly no little feather and no drop of red blood fell. When she raised her eyes, the dove had dis-appeared. She thought to herself, "No one can help me now." She climbed up over a peak to get closer to the sun. "Have you seen a white dove flying?"

"No," said the sun. "I have seen none, but I will give you a small box. Open it when you are in sorest need."

She thanked the sun and went on until evening came and the moon appeared. She asked the moon, "You shine the whole night through on every field and forest. Have you seen a white dove flying?"

"No," said the moon. "I have seen no dove, but here I will give you an egg. Break it when you are in great need."

She thanked the moon and went on until the night wind came up and blew on her. Then she said to it, "You blow over every tree and under every leaf. Have you seen a white dove flying?"

"No," said the night wind. "I have seen none, but I will ask the three other winds. Perhaps they have seen it." The east wind and the west wind came and had seen nothing. The south wind said, "I have seen the white dove. It has flown to the Red Sea. There it has become a lion again. The seven years are over and the lion is there fighting with a dragon. The dragon, however, is an enchanted princess."

The night wind then told her, "I will advise you. Go to the Red Sea. On the right bank are some tall reeds. Count them, break off the eleventh and strike the dragon with it. Then the lion will be able to subdue it and both of them will regain their human form. After that, look around and you will see the griffin by the Red Sea. Swing yourself with your beloved, on to his back and the bird will carry you over the sea to your own home. Here is a nut for you. When you are above the center of the sea, let the nut fall. It will immediately shoot up, and a tall nut tree will grow out of the water on which the griffin may rest. If he cannot rest, he will not be strong enough to carry you across. If you forget to throw down the nut, he will let you fall into the sea."

The lion prince's wife followed the directions and found everything as the night wind had said. She counted the reeds by the sea and cut off the eleventh, struck the dragon with it, and the lion overcame it. Immediately, both the lion and the dragon regained their human shapes. The dragon princess swiftly took the prince by the arm, seated herself on the griffin, and carried him off with her.

The poor maiden who had wandered so far stood there forsaken. She sat down and cried. Finally regaining her courage, she said, "Still I will go as far as the wind blows and as long as the cock crows, until I find him." She went forth by long, long roads, until at last she came to the castle where both of them had lived together. There, she heard that soon there was to be a feast to celebrate the wedding of the princess and the prince.

"I will not fail now," she said to herself and opened the little box the sun had given her. A dress lay inside as brilliant as the sun itself. When she put it on and went up into the castle, everyone, even the bride herself, looked at her with astonishment.

The dress pleased the cruel bride so well that she thought it might do for her wedding dress and asked if it were for sale. "Not for money or land," answered the maiden. "Only for flesh and blood."

"What do you mean?" asked the bride.

"Let me stay a night in the room where the bridegroom sleeps," answered the maiden. The bride would not, yet she dearly wanted the dress. At last she consented, but unknown to the maiden, she had given the bridegroom a sleeping potion.

When it was night, the young man was in a deep sleep. She entered his room and sat herself on the bed. "I have followed you for seven years. I have been to the sun and the moon and the four winds. I have inquired for you and have helped you against the dragon. Will you now forget me?" But the prince slept soundly and in his dreams he only heard the wind whistling outside in the fir trees.

When morning came, the maiden was led out and had to give up the golden dress. Sadly she went to a meadow, sat down there, and wept. Then, she remembered the egg that the moon had given her. She opened it and out came a clucking hen with twelve chickens, all of gold. They ran about chirping and crept again under the old hen's wings. There was nothing more beautiful ever seen in the world! The maiden arose and drove them through the meadow before her until the bride looked out of the window. The little gold chickens pleased her so much that she immediately came down and asked if they were for sale.

"Not for money or land. Only for flesh and blood," replied the maiden. "Let me stay another night in the room where the bridegroom sleeps."

Thinking it over, the bride agreed. "Yes," she said, planning to cheat the maiden as on the former evening.

When the prince went to bed, he asked the page, "What is the murmuring and rustling I heard in the last night?" The page told him everything.

"I was forced to give you a sleeping potion," he said. "A poor maiden stayed secretly in your room last night. I am to give you another potion tonight."

The prince thought and then said to the page, "Pour out the potion by the bed and empty it on the floor."

That night, the maiden was again led into the room. They looked at each other and she related what had happened. He, of course, recognized her, sprang up, and cried, "Now, I am really released! I have been as if in a dream for the strange princess had bewitched me. Your memory was driven from me. But, dear wife, you have persevered and delivered me from the spell."

They both left the castle secretly in the night for they feared the father of the evil princess, who was a sorcerer. They seated themselves on the griffin, which bore them across the Red Sea. When they were in the midst of it, she let fall the nut, and immediately a tall tree grew up. The bird rested on it and then after being refreshed, carried them home. They found their child who had grown tall and beautiful, and lived happily until their death many years later.

Thoughts About the Stories, Discussions, and Activities

ROBERT THE BRUCE, THE KING

This is the story of a real person and the lesson he learned from observing a humble spider.

⊙ *Consider the story of "Robert the Bruce." Most of us aren't faced with such an extreme situation, but we can use perseverance in other ways. What are some of the ways we can learn to develop patience and persistence in our daily lives?*
⊙ *Research Robert the Bruce in the library or on the Internet and write a brief biography of him.*
⊙ *Make a list of some of the other leaders in history or in contemporary life that have demonstrated heroism through perseverance.*

THE STORYTELLER

This is another story of how simple patience and persistence can show us how to win good fortune.

⊙ *The story ends with the statement, "one grain at a time brings good fortune." What does this mean to you? How does it relate to the phrase "practice makes perfect"?*

⊙ *Do you know of any instances in your life where a simple or poor person outwitted a powerful, greedy one? Share these stories.*

THE DRAGON AND THE PRINCE

This tale uses the formula of three sons, with the youngest one being humble, helpful, and able to win out over danger and dragons.

⊙ *Why do you think the youngest son was the only one to succeed in this story?*
⊙ *Many folktales feature dragons. What do they generally represent? Research dragons in the library or on the Internet and draw an illustration of one to accompany this story.*

THE SINGING, SOARING LARK

This story examines the values of the king's three daughters, particularly the youngest one, along with keeping our promises even though they may seem disastrous.

⊙ *What are some of the symbols you can find in this story? How do they relate to perseverance?*

Other Activity Ideas

⊙ Reflect on the following quotes from over the ages. Why do you think there are so many? Discuss what they have to say about the value of perseverance and hard work:

  ⊙ "Work is the sustenance of noble minds." (Seneca)
  ⊙ "There is no substitute for hard work." (Thomas Edison)
  ⊙ "Even in the meanest sorts of labor, the whole soul of man is composed into a kind of real harmony the instant he sets himself to work." (Thomas Caryle)
  ⊙ "Honor lies in honest toil." (Grover Cleveland)
  ⊙ "The gods sell us all good things for hard work." (Epicharmus)

⊙ Write about an experience you have had when perseverance paid off.

⊙ Do animals teach us about perseverance? List some examples.

⊙ Research at your school or public library pieces of literature that are concerned with a character persevering. Share with others.

⊙ Sing the song "High Hopes." Create new verses on the same theme.

⊙ Make a list of things that motivate you to keep trying. How many are extrinsic (money, M&M's)? Compare these with intrinsics that help you feel good and are beneficial.

⊙ *Question your parents and other adults about times when persevering produced positive results for them. Write an essay on perseverance.*

⊙ *Are all tasks interesting and intriguing? What helps us persevere and complete those that are not? How does perseverance relate to completing homework or assignments? Collect stories from the newspaper about people who persevere and create a scrapbook with others in the class.*

⊙ *Review the* Guinness Book of Records *for examples of people who persevered. Discuss when it is appropriate to give up and how it feels. What famous sports figures, politicians, musicians, and actors are known for not giving up? Research one of these individuals and write a short biography about him or her.*

⊙ *The finger-play rhyme and song of the itsy, bitsy spider and the water spout tells of the rain washing the spider back down to the ground, of the sun emerging, drying up the rain, and then the spunky little spider becoming a model of perseverance. Discuss with others how this rhyme might influence youngsters with their thinking. Organize a session with kindergarten/first graders in which you enact the rhyme and query the youngsters as to the meaning of the song/game. Did any of them make a connection with the spider continuing in its efforts and finally succeeding?*

See the "General Activities" section at the back of this book for more ideas to further explore these topics.

Trustworthiness

The Lute Player
(Russia)

Once upon a time there were a king and queen who lived happily and comfortably together. They were deeply in love, respected one another, and had nothing to worry them, but still the king grew restless. He longed to go out into the world to do good things, to try his strength in battle against some enemy, and to win all kinds of honor and glory. So he called his army together and gave orders to leave for a distant country where a wicked king ruled and mistreated or tormented everyone within his power. The king then gave parting orders and wise advice to his ministers, took a tender leave of his wife, and set off with his army across the sea.

It is not known whether the voyage was short or long, but at last the king reached the country of the wicked king and marched on, defeating all who challenged him. However, he soon came to a mountain pass, where a large army was waiting for him. They put his soldiers to flight, and captured the king himself. He was carried off to the prison where the wicked king kept his captives, and now the poor king had a very bad time indeed. All night long the prisoners were chained up, and in the morning they were yoked together like oxen and forced to plough the land till it grew dark.

This went on for three years before the king found any means of sending news of himself to his dear queen, but at last he contrived to send this letter: "Sell all our castles and palaces, and put all our treasures in pawn and come and deliver me out of this horrible prison."

The queen received the letter, read it, and wept bitterly as she said to herself, "How can I deliver my dearest husband? If I go myself and the wicked king sees me, he will just take me to be one of his wives. If I were to send one of the ministers!—but I hardly know if I can depend on them." She thought and thought, and at last an idea came into her head. She cut off all her beautiful long brown hair and dressed herself in boy's clothes. Then she took her lute and, without saying anything to anyone, she went forth into the wide world.

It is not known whether it was a long or short time, but she traveled through many lands, saw many cities, and went through many hardships before she got to the town where the wicked king lived. When she arrived, she walked all around the palace and saw the prison at the back. Then she went into the great court in front of the palace, and with her lute began to play so beautifully that one could never hear enough.

After she had played for some time, she began to sing, and her voice was sweeter than the lark's:

> I come from my own country far
> Into this foreign land,
> Of all I own I take alone
> My sweet lute in my hand.
>
> Oh! who will thank me for my song,
> Reward my simple lay?
> Like lovers' sighs it still shall rise
> To greet thee day by day.
>
> I sing of blooming flowers
> Made sweet by sun and rain;
> Of all the bliss of love's first kiss,
> And parting's cruel pain.
>
> Of the sad captive's longing
> Within his prison wall,
> Of hearts that sigh when none are nigh
> To answer to their call.
>
> My songs beg for your pity,
> And gifts from out your store,
> And as I play my gentle lay
> I linger near your door.

And if you hear my singing
Within your palace, sire,
Oh! give, I pray, this happy day,
To me my heart's desire.

No sooner had the wicked king heard this touching song sung by such a lovely voice, than he had the singer brought before him.

"Welcome, O lute player," said he. "Where do you come from?"

"My country, sire, is far away across many seas. For years I have been wandering about the world and gaining my living by my music."

"Stay here then a few days, and when you wish to leave I will give you what you ask for in your song—your heart's desire."

So the queen stayed in the palace and sang and played almost all day long to the king, who could never tire of listening and almost forgot to eat, drink, or torment people. He cared for nothing but the music, and nodded his head as he declared, "That's something like playing and singing. It makes me feel as if some gentle hand had lifted every care and sorrow from me."

After three days, the queen came to take leave of the king.

"Well," said the king, "What do you desire as your reward?"

"Sire, give me one of your prisoners. You have so many in your prison, and I should be glad of a companion on my journeys. When I hear his happy voice as I travel along I shall think of you and thank you."

"Come along then," said the king, "choose whom you will." And he took her through the prison himself.

The queen walked about among the prisoners, and at length she picked out her husband and took him with her on her journey. It is not known whether they traveled a long or short time, but he never found out who she was, as she led him nearer and nearer to his own country.

When they reached the frontier, the king said, "Let me go now, kind lad. I am no common prisoner, but the king of this country. Let me go free and ask what you will as your reward."

"Do not speak of reward," answered the queen. "Go in peace."

"Then come with me, dear boy, and be my guest."

"When the proper time comes I shall be at your palace," was the reply, and so they parted.

The queen took a short way home, got there before the king, and changed her dress.

An hour later, all the people in the palace were running to and fro and crying out, "Our king has come back! Our king has returned to us."

The king greeted everyone very kindly, but he could not so much as look at the queen.

Then he called all his council and ministers together and said to them, "See what sort of a wife I have. Here she is falling on my neck, but when I was pining in prison and sent her word of it, she did nothing to help me." His council answered with one voice, "Sire, when news was brought from you, the queen disappeared and no one knew where she went. She only returned today."

Then the king was very angry and cried, "Judge my faithless wife! Never would you have seen your king again if a young lute player had not delivered him. I shall remember him with love and gratitude as long as I live."

While the king was sitting with his council, the queen found time to disguise herself. She took her lute, and slipping into the court in front of the palace she sang, clear and sweet:

> I sing the captive's longing
> Within his prison wall,
> Of hearts that sigh when none are nigh
> To answer to their call.
>
> My song begs for your pity,
> And gifts from out your store,
> And as I play my gentle lay
> I linger near your door.
>
> And if you hear my singing
> Within your palace, sire,
> Oh! give, I pray, this happy day,
> To me my heart's desire.

As soon as the king heard this song, he ran out to meet the lute player, took the queen by the hand and led her into the palace. "Here," he cried, "is the boy who released me from my prison. And now, my true friend, I will indeed give you your heart's desire."

"I am sure you will not be less generous than the wicked king was sire. I ask of you what I asked and obtained from him. But this time I don't mean to give up what I get. I want you—yourself!"

And as she spoke, she threw off her long cloak and everyone saw it was the queen.

Who can tell how happy the king was? With the joy of his heart he gave a great feast, and the whole world came and rejoiced with him for a whole week.

I was there too, and ate and drank many good things. I shan't forget that feast as long as I live.

The Wonderful Hair
(Slavonic)

There was a man who was very poor, but rich in children; so rich, in fact, that he was utterly unable to feed and clothe them. He became desperate, and more than once thought of killing them so he wouldn't see their misery in dying of hunger. His wife made him admit how even though they were all starving, he could not follow through with his plan.

One night, a child came to him in his sleep and said: "Man! I see that you have considered destroying your poor little children. I know how desperate and depressed you are, but in the morning you will find under your pillow a mirror, a red kerchief, and an embroidered pocket handkerchief. Take all three of these secretly and tell nobody.

"Go to the hill I will describe to you and near it you will find a stream. Go along the stream until you come to its beginnings. There you will find a maiden as bright as the sun with her hair hanging down over her back. Be sure to be on your guard and keep the ferocious she-dragon from coiling around you. Do not converse with her if she speaks. The reason for that is that if you converse with her, she will poison you and turn you into a fish or something else. Then it will devour you.

"If she bids you examine her head, examine it and as you turn over her hair, look and you will find one hair as red as blood. Pull it out and run back again. If she suspects and begins to run after you, throw her the kerchief and lastly, the mirror. Then she will be diverted by these items. Sell that red hair to some rich man.

But, be careful that they don't cheat you because they will try. That hair is worth countless wealth. In this way, you will get riches to maintain yourself and your children."

When the poor man woke, he found everything under his pillow that the child in his dreams had told him about. Then he went to the hill, searched, and found the stream. He continued alongside of it until he came to the stream's beginning. Looking carefully about him, he finally saw the maiden above a piece of water that shone like sunbeams threaded on a needle. The maiden sat at a frame embroidering on stuff, the threads of which were young men's hair.

As soon as he saw the maiden, the poor man bowed low and demonstrated great respect for her. She stood up and questioned him, "Who are you, unknown young man?"

He held his tongue and did not answer her.

She questioned him again, "Who are you? Why have you come?" but he was as mute as a stone, making signs with his hands as if he were deaf and needed help.

She told him to sit down on her skirt. He did not wait for any more orders and sat down. When she bent her head toward him, he turned over her hair as if to examine it. He immediately found the red strand, quickly separated it and pulled it out, then jumped off her skirt and ran away as best he could.

The maiden realized what had happened and followed full speed after him. He looked around and seeing that she was about to overtake him, he threw the embroidered pocket-handkerchief, as he had been told. When she saw the pocket-handkerchief, she stooped and began to inspect it in every direction. She admired the embroidery until he had traveled a good way off. Then the maiden placed the pocket-handkerchief in her dress and ran after him again.

When he saw that she was again at his heels, he threw the red kerchief. She stopped, picked it up, admired and studied it until the poor man had again made it a good way off.

Then the girl became exasperated and threw both the pocket-handkerchief and the kerchief away, and ran after the poor man in full pursuit.

Again, when he saw that she was about to overtake him, he threw the mirror. When the maiden came to the mirror, the likes of which she had never seen before, she lifted it up. Not realizing that she was the image in the mirror, she fell in love with the reflection of herself.

The man got so far off that she was no longer able to overtake him and realizing this, she turned back. When the man reached his home safe and sound, he showed his wife the hair and told her everything that had happened to him. She began to jeer and laugh at him, but he paid no attention to her and went to town to sell the hair.

A crowd of all sorts of people and merchants collected around him. One offered a sequin, another two, and so on, higher and higher until they came to 100 gold sequins.

Just then, the emperor heard of the hair and he summoned the man into his presence. The emperor said, "I will give you a thousand sequins for the hair!" and the man sold it to him. What was the hair? The emperor split it in two from top to bottom and found many remarkable things registered there in writing. These were things that had happened in the olden times since the beginning of the world.

Thus, the man became rich and lived well with his wife and children. The child who had come to him in his sleep was an angel sent from heaven to aid the poor man and to reveal unimaginable secrets.

Ananzi and the Lion
(Africa)

Once upon a time, Ananzi planned a scheme. He went to town and bought ever so many pounds of fat, numerous sacks, several balls of string, and a very big frying pan. Then he went to the bay and threw a shell, calling to the head fish in the sea, Green Eel. He said to the fish, "The King sends me to tell you that you must bring all the fish on shore for he wants to give them new life."

Green Eel said he would, and went to call them. Meanwhile, Ananzi lit a fire and took out some of the fat. He got his frying pan ready, and as fast as the fish came out of the water he caught them and put them into the frying pan. He did this with each of them until he got to the head fish, which was so slippery that he couldn't hold it. Green Eel slipped out of Ananzi's hands and got back again into the water.

When Ananzi had fried all the fish, he put them into the sacks, and set off to the mountains with the sacks on his back. He hadn't gone very far when he met Lion. "Well brother Ananzi, where have you been? I have not seen you for a long time," said Lion.

Ananzi replied, "I have been traveling about."

"But what have you got there?" Lion asked.

"Oh! I have got my mother's bones—she has been dead these forty-eleven years and they say I must not keep her here. That is why I am taking her up into the middle of the mountains to bury her." They parted, but after he had gone a little way, Lion said to himself, "I know that Ananzi is a great rogue. I dare say he has got something there that he doesn't want me to see. I will just follow him." As he went, Lion took care not to let Ananzi see him.

When Ananzi got into the wood, he set his sacks down, took one fish out, and began to eat. Then a fly came and Ananzi said, "I cannot eat any more for there is someone near." He tied the sack up and went on farther into the mountains where he set his sacks down. He took out two fish, which he ate. No fly came. Ananzi said, "There is no one near," so he took out more fish. When he had eaten about half a dozen, Lion came up and said, "Well, brother Ananzi, a pretty tale you have told me."

"Oh! Brother Lion. I am so glad you have come. Never mind what tale I have told you but come and sit down—it was only my fun." So Lion sat down and began to eat, but before Ananzi had eaten two fish, Lion had emptied one of the sacks. Ananzi said to him, "Greedy fellow, you are eating up all my fish."

"What do you say, sir?" asked Lion, with his eyes squinting.

"I only said you do not eat half fast enough," said Ananzi, afraid Lion would eat him up.

They went on eating, but Ananzi wanted to revenge himself and he said, "Which of us do you think is the stronger?"

"Why, I am, of course," replied Lion.

Then Ananzi said, "We will tie one another to the tree and see which is the stronger."

They agreed that Lion should tie Ananzi first. He tied him loosely with some very fine string that broke after Ananzi twisted himself about two or three times.

When it was Ananzi's turn to tie Lion, he took some very strong cord. Lion said, "You must not tie me tight for I did not tie you tight."

Ananzi said, "Oh! No, to be sure, I will not." But he tied him as tight as ever he could, then told Lion, "Try and get loose." Lion tried and tried in vain—he could not get loose. Ananzi thought, "now is my chance," so he got a big stick and beat Lion. Then Ananzi was afraid that if he loosened the cord, Lion would kill him, so he went away and left him tied up.

There was a woman called Miss Nancy, who was going out one morning to get some "callalou" (spinach) in the wood. As she went along, she heard someone say, "Good morning, Miss Nancy!" At first she could not tell who spoke to her. Then, she looked in the direction of the voice and saw Lion tied to the tree.

"Good morning, Mr. Lion. What are you doing there?" she asked.

Lion told her, "It is that fellow Ananzi who has tied me to the tree. Will you loose me?"

She said, "No, for I am afraid if I do you will kill me." He gave her his word he would not. Still she could not trust him. He begged her again and again.

Lion pleaded, "Well, if I do try to eat you, I hope all the trees will cry out shame upon me."

At last she consented, but she had no sooner loosed him than he attempted to eat her. "I have been many days without food and am quite ravenous," he said.

The trees immediately cried out, "Shame!" Of course he could not eat her then.

Miss Nancy went away as fast as she could and Lion found his way home. When he arrived, he told his wife and children all that had happened to him. "Miss Nancy saved my life." His family said they would have a great dinner and invite Miss Nancy. When Ananzi heard of this, he wanted to go to the dinner. He went to Miss Nancy and told her, "You must take me with you as your child to Lion's dinner."

She said, "No!"

Ananzi begged, "I can turn myself into quite a little child and then you can take me."

After his repeated pleadings, she agreed. "When they ask you what food your baby eats, be sure to tell them it eats the same food as everyone else." They went and had a very good dinner, then set off for home again. But somehow one of Lion's sons felt that all was not right. When he told his father, "I am sure that baby was Ananzi," Lion set out after them.

As they walked along, Ananzi begged Miss Nancy to put him down so he could run. When she did, he ran away along the wood. Lion spotted him and chased him. When Ananzi saw that Lion was overtaking him, he turned himself into an old man with a bundle of wood on his head. When Lion caught up to him, he said, "Good morning, Mr. Lion."

"Good morning, old gentleman," answered Lion.

The old man asked, "What are you after now?"

"Have you seen Ananzi pass that way?" Lion asked.

"No," the old man said, "that fellow Ananzi is always meddling with someone. What mischief has he been up to now?"

Lion told him, but the old man said it was no use to follow him anymore, for he would never catch him. So, Lion wished him "Good day," turned, and went home again.

The Boy Who Cried Wolf
(Aesop)

A shepherd boy was tending to his flock of sheep near a village. He thought it would be great fun to fool the villagers by pretending that a wolf was attacking the sheep.

He shouted out, "Wolf! Wolf!" When the people came running up to him, he laughed at them for their pains. He did this more than once, and each time the villagers found that they had been tricked.

Finally, one day a wolf really did come and again the boy cried, "Wolf! Wolf!" as loudly as he could. But by then the villagers were so used to hearing him trick them by calling "Wolf!" that they paid no attention to his cries for help. And so the wolf had the flock to his own doing, killing off one sheep after another at his leisure.

The Donkey in the Lion's Skin
(Aesop)

A donkey once found a lion's skin that some hunters had left out in the sun to dry. He put it on and trotted through the forest and meadow scaring all the poor animals that saw him.

The donkey was so proud of himself that he raised his head and brayed loudly in triumph. A wily fox heard him and immediately recognized him as a donkey.

"I'm very sorry, my friend," said the fox. "It doesn't pay to pretend to be what you aren't. You may pretend to be a lion but you are still a donkey!"

The Glencoe Massacre
(Scotland—A True Story)

Like individuals, governments and political factions are either trustworthy or not. One cruel case in point is the Glencoe Massacre of February 13, 1692.

Glencoe is located in a lovely valley of the Scottish Highlands. This area is one of massive splendor, with towering peaks and mysterious clouds that ooze over the mountains and down to the valley. It was the home to goats that scrambled on the mountains, eagles that soared majestically above, and a little-used military road that passed through the valley. A river rushed and dashed over its rugged bed and the noise of the torrents that poured in from the mountainsides provided the song of rapid waters.

This massacre in 1692 nearly annihilated a Highland clan. It had been decreed that all the Highlanders were required to take an oath of allegiance to English King William III before the year 1691 was over. Every clan did so with the exception of the MacDonalds of Glencoe. Their old chief had held out until the last moment, then realizing that he had been foolish, the old man set off through the snowdrifts to swear loyalty before the magistrates at Fort William.

When the chief arrived there, he discovered that the oath should be taken before the sheriff at Inveraray. The old man went on through the harsh weather. The passes were deep in snow, the wind was bitter, and he did not reach Inveraray until January 6. He took the oath and the sheriff reported to the authorities at Edinburgh that the Clan MacDonald had fallen into line.

Then intrigue built as Sir John Dalrymple, secretary of state, plotted to wipe out the MacDonalds. It was therefore no surprise that when the register arrived to the Privy Council in Edinburgh, the name of MacDonald of Glencoe had been obliterated and the clan officially liable for punishment.

Dalrymple wrote to a friend in Scotland expressing delight "that the time of grace expired in the depth of winter because that is the proper season to maul them, in the cold, long nights." He wrote to the commander in chief on January 11, "My Lord Argyll tells me that Glencoe hath not taken the oaths at which I rejoice—it is a great work of charity to exact in rooting out that damnable sect, the worst in all of the Highlands."

So English forces aided by political power-seeking Scotsmen planned to punish the MacDonalds. At the beginning of February, four weeks after old MacDonald had taken the oath, a detachment of 120 men of the Earl of Argyll's regiment—all Campbells and hereditary enemies of the MacDonalds—set out from the garrison at Inverlochy under the command of the Campbells. Robert Campbell of Glenlyon, one of those in the detachment, ironically was a relative by marriage of the old chief's. The troops marched through the snows and into the valley, where the MacDonalds received them with true Highland hospitality. Again, ironically, the murderers and victims settled down together.

Daily, the commander called on the old chief at his home. They played cards, ate and drank together. The whole time this was going on, Campbell had in his pocket the savage death-knell for the clan that read: "You are to put all to the sword under seventy. (These words were underlined.) You are to have a special care that the old fox and his son do on no account escape your hands. You are to secure all avenues that none escape. You are to start the execution at precisely five o'clock in the morning. I will strive to arrange for a stronger party to help. Whatever happens, you are not to tarry for me, but to fall on."

The MacDonald clan had hosted the Campbell men for twelve days. On the eve of the planned massacre, the Campbell forces housed throughout the village still accepted their hospitality.

At five o'clock on that dark winter morning, the signal was given and the foul massacre began. Throughout the valley, each "guest" murdered the host and his family in their home. The old chief was shot as he got out of bed. The whole glen echoed with the cries of the murdered and the shots of the murderers. Some MacDonalds tried to escape through the snow and over the mountains.

In the morning light, the snow was bloody and the smoke of the burning houses floated skyward in the frosty air. Thirty-eight MacDonalds had been murdered. As long as the hills stand, people will remember Glencoe and the unparalleled atrocity that took place.

The following song, "The Glencoe Massacre," was printed on broad-sheets and in chapbooks and is probably not older that the nineteenth century. The words of the song bring a very human aspect to the massacre.

O, dark loured the night o'er the wild mountain heath,
The wild raven's croaked out the bodings of death,
While Flora, poor Flora, she wander'd in woe,
To seek for MacDonald, the pride of Glencoe.

While sweet balmy sleep closed each eye in rest,
And the chieftain slumbered with peace in his breast,
Ne'er dreading the hour that fate seem'd to show,
That bloody and pale he should lie in Glencoe.

But a flash soon denoted the signal was given,
And the thunders of death wak'd the meteors of Heav'n,
While Flora, poor Flora, she wander'd in woe,
To seek for MacDonald the pride of Glencoe.

Oh! Sudden a flash on her vision did glare,
While a cannon's loud thunder was pealed through the air,
It wakened ten thousand brave heroes below,
And roared through the caverns of mighty Glencoe.

The smoke then arose from our dear native glen,
With the shrieks of the women and the cries of the men,
Naked mothers were shot with their babes as they ran,
For the English had risen to murder the clan.

Oh, many a warrior that evening was slain,
While the blaze of the village gleam'd far o'er the plain,
Helpless MacDonalds that night were laid low,
And their blood stained the heath of their native Glencoe.

Then Flora she shriek'd while loose hung her hair,
O, where is my Donald, O tell me, O where;
The tempest's loud torrents o'er the mountains do blow;
And stretch'd cold and bloody he lies in Glencoe.

With a sigh of despair then arose from her breast,
And memory soon told her he slumbered at rest,
He slumbers forever now free from his woe,
And left his loved Flora, the pride of Glencoe.

Her dark rolling eyes then did kindle like fire,
She fell on his body and then did expire;
No more lovely Flora again feared her woe,
But in death found her Donald, the pride of Glencoe.

Now over their heads the green grass does wave,
And the wild flowers do nod o'er their desolate grave,
And the strangers at the pass shed a tear as they go,
For Flora and Donald, the pride of Glencoe.

The Monkey and the Dolphin
(Aesop)

Sometimes when people go on a trip they take pets along with them for comfort. So it was long ago that a man returning to Athens from the East had a pet monkey on board the ship with him. As they neared the coast of Attica, a great storm boiled upon them and the boat capsized. Everyone and everything on board was thrown into the water. People tried to save themselves by swimming, as did the monkey.

A dolphin saw the monkey and, thinking him to be a man, took him on his back and began swimming toward the shore. When they got near the Piraeus, which is the port of Athens, the dolphin asked the monkey, "Are you an Athenian?"

"I am," was the monkey's reply. "In fact, I come from a very distinguished family."

"Then of course, you know the Piraeus," said the dolphin.

The monkey was confused, and thinking the dolphin referred to some high official or other, answered, "Oh, yes, he is a very old and dear friend of mine."

At that, the dolphin recognized the monkey's lie and was so disgusted that he dove below the surface. The startled monkey was swept out to sea and quickly drowned.

Thoughts About the Stories, Discussions, and Activities

THE LUTE PLAYER

This is a story of loyalty. The king doesn't trust his wife to plan and execute his release from prison.

- ☉ *If the situation were switched between husband and wife in this story, do you think the wife would trust her husband?*
- ☉ *What is a lute? What do you think it symbolizes in this story? Research the lute in the library or on the Internet and write a report on your findings.*

THE WONDERFUL HAIR

This hopeful story of belief and serendipity demonstrates that even when logic tells us something is hopeless, following our instincts leads to victory.

- ☉ *This story begins by saying there was a man who was poor, but rich in children. What does this mean? Are children assets to their parents? Why or why not?*
- ☉ *In this story, a single strand of hair leads to untold wealth. What do you suppose the message is behind this turn of events?*

ANANZI AND THE LION

In this story, we look at the mischief makers who cannot be trusted.

- *We all have met troublemakers such as in "Ananzi and the Lion." Do you know anyone who is satisfied only when making trouble and who does not keep his word? What is the best way to deal with such a person?*
- *There are many stories about Ananzi. Go to the library and see if you can find others in folktale collections or picture books.*

THE BOY WHO CRIED WOLF

This fable has become part of our language and is used sometimes to quickly draw attention to behavior that is unsatisfactory.

- *At the end of this story, the boy is no longer trusted. What does this tell us about earning someone's trust?*
- *Create an illustrated version of this tale in comic-strip form. End the strip with the statement "And the moral of the story is:" filling in the rest of the sentence.*

THE DONKEY IN THE LION'S SKIN

This is a quick lesson on being yourself and not pretending otherwise.

- *Have you ever pretended to be something you weren't and then were found out? What gave you away? Write a story about the experience.*

THE GLENCOE MASSACRE

This story tells us a piece of Scotland's history. People with political power committed barbaric acts and left a legacy of shame behind them.

- *Research the Glencoe Massacre in the library or on the Internet. Identify on a map of Scotland where this happened.*
- *What is an "oath of allegiance"? Do people make such oaths today, and if so, do they guarantee trustworthiness? Why or why not?*
- *Recite the words to the song "The Glencoe Massacre" as a group, with different individuals reading separate verses.*

⊙ *Compare the Glencoe Massacre to another similar historic event (e.g., the bombing of the World Trade Center, the Jewish Holocaust).*

THE MONKEY AND THE DOLPHIN

Here is a clever look at characters that aren't truthful, but instead full of ego.

⊙ *In this story, a monkey lies in order to make an impression. When lies are found out, what is the normal consequence?*
⊙ *What is a "white lie"? Did the monkey tell a "white lie"? Are "white lies" acceptable? Discuss.*

Other Activity Ideas

- Can we trust people who are chronic flatterers? What might they really say behind our backs?
- Have you ever heard or read the story of George Washington cutting down the cherry tree? What does this story teach about Washington's trustworthiness? Is it a true story or a legend? Research this in the library or on the Internet and discuss your findings.
- Abraham Lincoln was another actual person with established values. Read the stories of his honesty in returning money to a customer from the store where he worked. Do actions really speak louder than words? Explain this.
- Read other stories of national heroes and heroines and list how they demonstrated their trustworthiness.
- Do other stories of real-life heroes and heroines compare or contrast to those from literature? Write an essay comparing a real-life hero to a fictional one.
- Following the September 11, 2001 tragedy in New York City, the firefighters and police were hailed as heroes. How did they earn this label? What was evident in their heroic efforts that qualified as trustworthiness? Discuss.
- What other people do you know who are trustworthy? Who are some other unsung heroes? Write a poem dedicated to "an unsung hero."
- What are the qualities of trustworthiness? Write an essay entitled, "Trustworthiness Is."

- *How does someone earn or build trust? Break trust?*

- *Mae Jemison, a forty-four-year-old doctor who became the first Black woman in space in 1992, wrote her autobiography,* Find Where the Wind Goes: Moments From My Life *(Scholastic Press, 2001). Read or listen to excerpts from this book and then talk about who you want to be, what obstacles could get in the way, and what could help you reach your dream. What does all of this say about being true to ourselves?*

- *A popular author of books for young readers, Tom (T. A.) Barron, has established the Gloria Barron Young Heroes Prize to celebrate Colorado's young heroes. He is looking for "young persons up to age 16 who have had to reach down deep inside to accomplish something, not just to survive but who have shown real courage and unselfishness to make their world better." Barron has received comments from his readers that the people in his books are real inspirations, to which he responds, "If imaginary heroes are a positive example, what effect would there be if we honored real live young people who have made a difference?" Borrow some of Barron's books from your library and identify the heroes and their actions.*

- *Can you conceive, organize, and lead an extraordinary activity that clearly benefits other people, our fellow creatures, or the planet we share? How? Imagine doing something great. What would be involved? Write your plans and discuss them with others.*

- *What does the quote, "Nature put the firewood there but every person must gather and light it themselves" have to say about initiating projects to inspire and develop trustworthiness?*

- *The Scottish writer Lord Byron is quoted below concerning heroes (from* Random House Webster's Quotationary, *Leonard Roy Frank, Editor, 1999). How do these comments relate to trustworthiness?*

  - *"The truly brave are soft of heart and yearn and feel for what their duty bids them do."*

  - *"Dreams in their development have breath and tears and tortures and the touch of joy. They leave a weight upon our waking thoughts. They take a weight from off our waking toils. They do divide our being. They become a portion of ourselves as of our time and look like heralds of eternity."*

  - *"He who ascends to mountain tops shall find the loftiest peaks most wrapt in clouds and snow. He who surpasses or subdues mankind must look down on the feelings of those below."*

- ⊚ *At your school or public library, look for other quotes from literary, scientific, or everyday people that relate to trustworthiness.*
- ⊚ *Find some examples of ordinary people being trustworthy in your local newspaper and create a scrapbook with others.*
- ⊚ *Joseph Campbell said, "We have not even to risk the adventure alone, for the heroes of all time have gone before us. The labyrinth is thoroughly known. We have only to follow the thread of the hero path," in an interview with Bill Moyers for "The Hero's Adventure" videotape issued by New York: Mystic Fire Video, 1988, which appeared as a television series. Again, what connects the heroes of the ages and trustworthiness? Write a profile of someone you trust and discuss this issue.*
- ⊚ *Rosa Parks became a symbol of civil rights activism. She demonstrated not only trustworthiness, but also self-confidence, respect, responsibility, fairness, love, and appreciation. Research in the library or on the Internet and read about her actions in the 1950s.*
- ⊚ *Study the biography of someone you trust and respect. Construct a biography poster to record significant information about that person. List all of their character traits. Note explanations of events in their life and what they have done to indicate their trustworthiness. Accompany this poster with an art project such as a portrait, collage, or sculpture. Incorporate art materials and techniques to enrich learning through all five senses. Share with others.*
- ⊚ *A person's trustworthiness is sometimes tested when he finds something of value. Should he return it to its owner or keep it? This is his moment of truth. When we're presented with moral choices, our dark sides may taunt us. Have you ever been tempted in such a situation? Keep an ongoing file of newspaper stories you discover in which the finder/finders return things of value to the owner. Organize a group to discuss these "Aha!" stories and share their thoughts about the finder's actions.*

See the "General Activities" section at the back of this book for ideas to further explore these topics.

Self-Discipline

Tiger's Whisker
(Korea)

Long ago, in ancient Korea, there was a time of warfare, battles, warriors, and those left behind waiting for it all to end. One particularly fierce warrior returned home from fighting battle after battle, for many years.

His wife greeted him with kisses, embraces, and tears of happiness. But the man who returned home wasn't the same as the man who had left years ago. He was now going through each day in a gloomy, detached way. There was no joy or liveliness left in his emaciated body. He didn't respond to his wife's relief and joy. In fact, all he did was sit at the table with his eyes cast down at his feet.

The wife told her husband what had happened since he had been gone, but he just sat there, unresponsive. He was not pleased when she placed all of his favorite foods before him; he just played with the food and pushed it away. In their bed at night, he turned his back to her and ignored her touch and attempts to comfort him. He curled himself up into a ball and just lay there. His wife didn't know how to reach him anymore. "What has happened dear husband? What can I do to help you? Please don't turn from me," she pleaded.

Her pleas had no effect on him. Finally, in total frustration, the wife went to the old wise man who healed people's sicknesses with potions and magical charms, as well as provided solutions to their problems. "What am I to do, oh wise one?" she begged. "My husband has returned from years of battle and he is not the same man I married. There is no love left in him."

The wise man listened to her story, stroked his beard, and thought for a while. "I may have the answer to your problem. You must win back your husband's love, but to do this, I will need some very special ingredients for the potion that will help you. I need the whisker of a fierce tiger. When you bring me such a whisker, I will mix the remedy."

The distraught wife stared at him in alarm. "What did you say? A tiger's whisker? A fierce tiger's whisker? I cannot get such a thing."

The old man placed one gnarled hand in his other and studied them. Then he said, "You must bring me what I need or I cannot help you win the love of your husband."

The warrior's wife didn't even thank the wise man for his guidance. She left his place and muttered to herself, "This is impossible. How am I to get the whisker of a fierce tiger and survive?" Then she got an idea. She went to the market and bought a chunk of fresh meat. Instead of returning home, she went into the jungle. She knew where the cave of the tiger was. From the sounds coming out of the cave, she knew the tiger was in there, sleeping. He slept in the mouth of the cave with the sun just reaching him. She walked softly, closer to the cave.

"Look how sharp his claws are," she thought. She sat down nearby and watched the heaving of the tiger's chest as he breathed in his sleep. After a while, she carefully set the chunk of meat on the rock where she had been sitting and softly left, returning home.

The next day, she did the same thing. For several weeks, she got meat, went to the cave, and each day left the meat a few inches closer to the sleeping tiger. Finally, the tiger, who was awake, didn't move as she approached him. He almost seemed to say, "Place the meat right in front of me."

More time passed, and the wife continued her daily trip to the tiger's cave. One daring time, she sat right next to the tiger. He watched her closely. More time passed and on one of the visits, she stretched her hand out, let the tiger sniff it, and then petted him. Several visits later, the tiger put his head near her lap and made a sound like a giant purr.

Many trips later, she carefully took a pair of tiny scissors from her pocket, leaned over to the tiger, and ever so carefully cut one of his whiskers.

She felt so victorious as she returned home with the tiger's whisker. She had done the impossible! Early the next morning, she trotted to the wise man's place and triumphantly gave him the whisker. "I did not forget your instructions. Here is the tiger's whisker that you need to make the magical potion that will win my husband's love back for me."

The wise old man accepted the whisker, studied it, and said, "hmmm, ah," and, "ooh." He turned it over in his fingers. Quietly he asked her, "How did you manage to get this tiger whisker?"

The wife answered, "At first, I thought it was an impossible task. Then I decided to try anyway. I knew where the tiger's cave was; I took a chunk of meat each day to him and patiently got closer to him each trip. I was very patient about it. We seemed to accept each other carefully and then we seemed to come to trust each other. It almost seemed like he let me cut his whisker like a precious gift."

What the wise old man did next shocked the wife. He threw the whisker into his cooking fire. "That is a wonderful story you have just told me," he said. The woman gasped.

"How could you throw the whisker in the fire? After all I have been through to get it? Why did you do such a thing?" the wife wailed. "Now how can you make the love potion for me?"

"Ah, dear patient one, you do not need magic and spells. Anyone who can tame a fierce animal like a tiger already knows how to win her husband's love. Just look at your husband and remember how you got the tiger to trust you," he advised.

And so, the wife returned home to her very unhappy husband. She no longer whimpered, whined, or scolded. She won his love again with her patience and gentleness. At long last, her warrior husband really returned to her.

The Magic Fish of Gold
(Finland)

There was once, we know not where, beyond seven times seven countries, and at a cock's crow even beyond them, an immense, tall, quivering birch tree. This birch tree grew long, seven times seventy-seven branches. On each branch there were seven times seventy-seven crow's nests, and in each nest, seven times seventy-seven young crows. It was in such a place that this story belongs.

There was once an old fisherman and his wife who lived by the shore of a clear blue lake in a small house made of logs. The man had fished in the nearby lakes for more than seven times seven years. His wife grew flax and wove cloth from her harvest. She also raised some sheep for their wool. Between the two of them, they ate well and were warmly dressed, and that was that.

One morning, the fishing was very poor. The old fisherman had caught nothing, but he decided to cast out his net one more time. This time, when he gathered in his net, he had one fish. Not just an ordinary fish, but one that was made of pure gold. Its fins were gold, its scales, eyes, and tail were gold.

"Ah, well, this special fish is better than nothing," he said to himself, and opened his birch-bark fish basket to put the gold fish in for the trip back home. "My wife will find pleasure in this beautiful fish." Just as he started to drop the gold fish into his basket, it began to implore him, "Put me back into the lake, old fisherman. If you do, I'll give you whatever you ask me! I'll reward you richly."

The old fisherman stroked his gray beard, and being a kind, gentle man, he carefully slid the fish back into the lake. "Enjoy, little fish. Go back where you belong."

When he returned home, his wife took his fish basket and looked in to see what he had caught that day. There was nothing in the basket. "How can this be? There are no fish for supper in here!" she grumbled.

"I was able to catch only one fish today, but it was a special one. It was pure gold and it talked. It promised to reward me richly if I returned it to the lake, so I took pity on it and let it swim free," he told her.

"What? You mean that you let such a wonderful fish escape? Why didn't you ask it for a house that has a roof without leaks?" she scolded him.

The fisherman didn't like it when his wife was cross with him, so he went back to the shore of the lake. "Golden fish, golden fish," he called out.

He saw the fish swim right up to the beach in front of him. "Why did you call me?" asked the fish.

"My wife wants a house that has a roof without leaks," explained the old fisherman. "Can you help us?"

"Go home. It is done," said the fish before it turned and disappeared into the lake.

When the fisherman got back home, lo and behold! Their log house had a new roof with sturdy beams and thick thatch on it.

Instead of being pleased, his wife scolded him even louder. "If the fish can do this, why don't you ask it for a fine new house with a separate room to sleep in?"

The old fisherman knew there would be no peace that night unless he did as she asked. He went back to the lake and called, "Golden fish, golden fish, I need you."

Just as before, the fish swam into the shallow water near the old man's feet. "You have called me. What do you want from me?" asked the fish.

"Forgive me, you amazing fish. I thank you for the new roof on our cabin, but now my wife wants a fine new house with a separate room to sleep in," the old man told him.

"Go home. It is done," said the fish and it turned, flipped its tail, and was off into the lake.

When he went back home he wasn't sure if he had taken a wrong turn, because where his log cabin used to be sat a beautiful red-painted house, with shutters, a porch, and curtains. Inside were a big kitchen and a large fireplace with a big chimney that had room in the back of it for a person to rest and get warm. There were fine curtains, rugs, and just as he had asked, a separate room to sleep in.

But his wife still wasn't satisfied. "You have no imagination, husband!" she shouted at him. "Why didn't you ask the fish for a castle? I don't want to be a peasant all my life! I want to be a fine lady with fancy clothes and jewelry. Why shouldn't we have a carriage with horses, too? I'm furious that you didn't think of asking for this." She threw a plate at him for emphasis. Luckily, he ducked and the plate smashed into the wall of the new house and flew into many pieces.

So, back to the shore of the lake he went. Would his wife never be happy? "Golden fish, golden fish, I really need your help."

With a ripple and a splash, the fish swam to the shore. "What is it, old fisherman? Why do you call me?"

The old man explained, "Please excuse me, dear fish, but my wife is crankier than I have ever seen her. She even threw a dish at me. Please excuse me, but I do need your help. Now she wants a castle, fine clothes, jewelry, a carriage, and horses. What am I to do?"

"Go home. It is all as you have asked," announced the fish as it jumped back into the lake.

Sure enough, when the old man got back to where his cabin had first been, then the house that replaced it, he found a fancy castle with several stories. He could see special places on the upper-story outside walls where he and his wife could have their own indoor facilities for toilet needs. He found his wife inside the castle sitting at a long carved wooden table in an elaborate padded chair sculptured with the faces of animals.

"I hope that you are happy now," he said. "What more could people such as us want?" He was sure that this would satisfy her. The windows even had glass in them to let in the light yet keep out the winds. The golden fish had given them riches beyond dreams.

Weeks went by, and his wife tried on all her new clothes, went for rides in her carriage, and grew more and more impatient. Then, as if she could hold it no longer, she exploded. "Is this the best that the fish can give us? As I ride around I see other people with great armies. I want bands that will constantly play music for us. I want stables of horses. I want the finest amber jewelry that there is. I want grand boats that travel around the lakes so that everyone can see that I am of highest royalty. I want bands to play music on the boats so that everyone can hear our joyous travel up and down the lakes." Her shrill shrieks could be heard throughout the castle.

As the old man walked back to the shore of the lake, he wondered how it all could have come to this. Was there no pleasing her? Where would her greed get them? But wearily he called out, "Golden fish, golden fish. Do not be angry, but my wife has sent me back to ask for yet more."

With a swish and a splash the fish appeared. "What is it this time, old man? What more could this wife of yours want?"

The old fisherman told the golden fish of his wife's latest demands. The fish stood on its tail, twirled around, and said, "Go home. It is done," as it dashed back into the lake.

Sure enough, before he even got home, he saw a huge boat with a band playing music that was loaded with people having a party out on the lake. And there was more. The old man had to make his way through enormous armies to get into the castle. There sat his wife, listening to a band playing marches and dance music. She was covered with amber necklaces, bracelets, rings, and earrings and even had amber beads hanging from her gown. Truly the fish had done all that was asked and more.

But again, this wasn't to be the end of it. His wife threw golden goblets at him and demanded that she become the mighty ruler of the lakes and rule over the golden fish. She wanted her castle to sit in the middle of the lake, rising to the sky. She demanded the power to raise storms that would strike terror into the hearts of people and beasts that beheld it. "You go tell the golden fish what I want!" she screamed. She was so furious that he did not dare to refuse her wishes.

At the shore, the trembling old fisherman became aware of a great storm raging in the lake. Waters billowed and roiled over the shore. Clouds burst forth walls of water. But still he called out, "Golden fish, golden fish. Hear my cry for help!"

Out of the storm appeared the golden fish, this time clearly angry. "What more could this woman possibly want? Has she no shame? What is it this time?"

The soggy, beaten old fisherman told the golden fish of his wife's new demands. "Forgive me, golden fish. . . ." he said as he bowed his head. Before the old man could finish what he was saying, the golden fish turned around, slapped his tail on the water, and slid back out into the deep.

When the old fisherman returned home, he found his old log cabin with the roof that leaked. On the doorstep sat his old wife dressed in her old patched and tattered clothes!

Note: Reprinted from The Enchanted Wood and Other Tales from Finland by Norma J. Livo and George O. Livo ©1999 Libraries Unlimited.

The Bag of Gold
(Finland)

There was once a poor woodsman who lived with his wife and children deep in the forest. They had a nice cozy log cabin that he had built himself. The woodcutter earned just enough money to keep them supplied with food—there was certainly no money left over for luxuries. However, he was a very sharing fellow with what little he had, and often fed hungry strangers and gave them shelter for the night when they needed it.

One cold day, a tired traveler stopped by and the woodsman invited him in to eat with them and spend the night. The stranger said, "There was a notice in the village I passed through this morning about a wood carving contest. The prize is to be a rich purse of gold. Woodcarvers from all over the country will vie for such a prize."

The woodsman told the stranger, "I am no woodcarver. I am sure there will be contestants with fantastic carvings of birds and animals, gnomes and trolls there. I couldn't begin to compete against such stiff competition."

"Try anyway," said the stranger with a curious twinkle in his eyes. The next morning, after a hearty breakfast, the stranger said, "Thank you very much for your warm kindness to a complete stranger," and he slung his pack on his shoulder and went on his way.

That evening after another long day of cutting wood in the forest, loading it up in his horse-drawn wagon, and getting it home, the woodsman's wife asked him, "Why don't you listen to the stranger and enter the competition?"

His children echoed her suggestion, "Yes, father. Do it, do it, do it."

He thought about it for a bit and then said to himself, "What do I have to lose?" After supper the woodsman sat in his comfortable chair by the fire and thought and thought. The rest of his family had gone to bed. The warmth of the fire made his eyes heavy and he fell asleep. In a dream, the stranger with the blue twinkling eyes appeared and whispered in his ear.

The next morning, the woodsman woke up with a start. He was still in his chair and the fire was now only a bed of warm embers. Remembering his dream, he took his axe and saw and went to the place in the forest where he logged his wood. In his dream the stranger had told him, "Go to the big stump of the old oak tree you cut down."

Following the stranger's direction, the woodsman cut the rest of the stump off and carried it home. Then he cut this part of the stump into a cube with its sides about an arm's length long. He planed and sanded each of the six sides to a fine polish and then varnished it until it sparkled, just like the stranger in his dream had told him to do.

In the morning after breakfast, he put his creation in a burlap sack and slung it over his shoulder. "I am off to the competition dear family." When he got to the village, he found that the judging had already gone on for quite a while and he was almost too late to enter the contest. A group of fat dignitaries, who he assumed were the judges, were going from one fantastic woodcarving to another.

"Hmmmm! This is a fine work of art!" said one. Others nodded their heads or occasionally shook their heads. "Ah," breathed another of the dignitaries as he looked at a bird carving with its outspread wings. Obviously, this group of men had to be the judges. They talked among themselves and went from object to object.

The woodcutter placed his creation on a table just as the men arrived. "What have you here?" they asked. The woodcutter unwrapped the burlap sack and carefully took out his gleaming wooden cube. The judges crowded around and examined the strange cube from every direction. They huddled around it in a group and whispered in a very animated way, nodding and gesturing. One judge placed his pointing finger on his lips, while another stood in awe with clasped hands behind his back.

Finally, the chief judge took his place to announce the winner. He held up the blue ribbon and went to the woodcutter's piece of work. He placed the winning ribbon on it, "This is the outstanding winner of the contest," he said as he shook the hand of the woodcutter. "You have just won a very prestigious first prize!"

All the other wood-carvers gathered around and oohed and aahed as they admired his work. "That is truly an amazing art object!" one declared. Another one claimed, "I have never ever seen anything so perfect—perfection in simplicity!" And yet, a third carver exclaimed, "This is certainly the work of a master! How could anyone carve such a magnificent thing?"

The woodcutter was awarded the fabulous bag of gold as his prize. Never did he dream that he would hold so much wealth in his hands. "We will give this winning carving to the king as a gift," announced the head of the judges, as he threw out his pudgy chest and placed his thumbs in his belt on either side of a large ornate silver belt buckle.

Back home, the woodsman and his family celebrated this grand good fortune with fine food and drink that he had brought home. They would never want again or wonder if there was enough food to go around.

And just what was his creation? It was an intricately tunneled cube of wood thanks to an army of wood-boring ants!

Thoughts About the Stories, Discussions, and Activities

TIGER'S WHISKER

This is a delightful, quiet example of overcoming fear and continuing to be positive in our seemingly impossible efforts to win with integrity and not wishful thinking.

⊙ *The wife in this story tried to please her husband to no avail. Have you ever been in such a situation? Discuss.*

⊙ *How did the wife exhibit self-discipline?*

THE MAGIC FISH OF GOLD

This story shows the common theme of greed and not accepting our blessings, but instead coveting what others have.

⊙ *Discuss how the wife and husband in this story both lack self-discipline. What traits do these characters exhibit?*

⊙ *Have you ever received a gift and wished for more? Write a story about it. Then rewrite the story as if what you received was exactly what you wanted. What insights did you gain from the writing?*

THE BAG OF GOLD

This story from Karelia, Finland, was told to George Livo many years ago by his father, Pekka Livo, who was born and raised there. It demonstrates creativity and discipline in art. True artists discipline themselves to see possibilities in common as well as uncommon objects.

⊙ *How did the woodsman exhibit self-discipline? What might an undisciplined person have done in his place?*

⊙ *Practice the discipline of observation. Make a list of all the beautiful objects in your immediate surroundings. Don't limit your list to pretty pictures and jewelry—you can include such items as a rusty pipe or a pile of laundry. Be as outrageous and creative as you can.*

Other Activity Ideas

- *Examples of the lack of self-discipline are all around us. Collect stories from newspapers in which there are examples of road rage, sideline rage, "postal rage," or other out-of-control behavior. Develop some role-playing situations in which you address how to avoid or act in such situations. Write a reader's theater script based on one of the situations and perform it.*

- *Identify and make a list of common everyday practices that demonstrate self-discipline (e.g., brushing your teeth). Share your list with others.*

- *Possibly included on your list were simple practices like having appropriate supplies ready for class. This seems like an easy task, but observe one day in your classes. How many times and ways did you detect people who were not prepared? Was homework done, did they have sharpened pencils, paper, and appropriate material ready?*

- *What professions require a lot of self-discipline? Consider the fields of religion and medicine.*

- *Which storybook characters (such as Winnie the Pooh, Peter Rabbit, or Ananzi) show lack of self-discipline? Which characters exhibit self-discipline? List them and explain why.*

- *Consider the adage, "anyone can be successful with hard work." Do you agree? How can self-discipline contribute to success? List as many ways as you can think of. Share your ideas with others who have also made lists. Compare similarities and differences.*

See the "General Activities" section at the end of this book for ideas to further explore these topics.

Self-Confidence

The Hummingbird
(China)

It was a hot, dampish day in the great Chinese jungle. Elephant was placing one foot in front of another and swinging his trunk as he traveled. Suddenly, this great beast saw a tiny bright hummingbird lying flat on its back on the ground.

The bird looked to be dead, for its two tiny feet were raised up into the air. It did not move at all; it just lay there with its feet pointing skyward.

The elephant moved close to the tiny bird and gave it a gentle nudge with his trunk.

"Do not push me around so," said the hummingbird.

"Then, you are not dead," said the worried elephant. "What on earth are you doing there like that? You could get trampled on."

The hummingbird opened his eyes to look up at the elephant. "I have heard that the sky might fall today. If that is really what is going to happen, I am ready to do my bit and help hold it up."

The elephant couldn't help laughing at this tiny optimistic creature. His laughter turned to mockery. "Come now, little bird, do you really think that those tiny feet of yours could possibly hold up the sky?"

The little bird looked up at this giant beast and quietly admitted, "No I could not probably do it all by myself, but every creature must do what it can do. And, this is what I can do!"

The Fifty-First Dragon
(An Original Story by Heywood Broun)

Of all the pupils at the knight school, Gawaine Le Coeur-Hardy was among the least promising. He was tall and sturdy, but his instructors soon discovered that he lacked spirit. He would hide in the woods when the jousting class was called, although his companions and members of the faculty sought to appeal to his better nature by shouting for him to come out and break his neck like a man. Even when they told him that the lances were padded, the horses no more than ponies, and the field unusually soft for late autumn, Gawaine refused to grow enthusiastic.

When the headmaster and the assistant professor of pleasance were discussing the case one spring afternoon, the assistant professor could see no remedy but expulsion.

"No," said the headmaster, as he looked out at the purple hills that encircled the school, "I think I'll train him to slay dragons."

"He might be killed," objected the assistant professor.

"So he might," replied the headmaster brightly, but then more soberly he added, "We must consider the greater good. We are responsible for the formation of this lad's character."

"Are the dragons particularly bad this year?" interrupted the assistant professor. This was characteristic; he always seemed restive when the head of the school began to talk ethics and ideals of the institution.

"I've never known them worse," replied the headmaster. "Up in the hills to the south last week they killed a number of peasants, two cows, and a prize pig. And if this dry spell holds, there's no telling when they may start a forest fire simply by breathing around indiscriminately."

"Would any refund on the tuition fee be necessary in case of an accident to young Coeur-Hardy?"

"No," the principal answered, judicially, "that's all covered in the contract. But as a matter of fact he won't be killed. Before I send him up in the hills I'm going to give him a magic word."

"That's a good idea," said the professor. "Sometimes they work wonders."

From that day on, Gawaine specialized in dragons. His course included both theory and practice. In the morning, there were long lectures on the history, anatomy, manners, and customs of dragons. Gawaine did not distinguish himself in these studies; he had a marvelously versatile gift for forgetting things. He showed to better advantage in the afternoon, however, when he would go down to the south meadow and practice with a battle-ax.

Gawaine was truly impressive in this exercise, for he had enormous strength as well as speed and grace. He even developed a deceptive display of ferocity. Old alumni say that it was a thrilling sight to see Gawaine charging across the field toward the dummy paper dragon that had been set up for his practice. As he ran, he would brandish his ax and shout, "A murrain on thee!" or some other vivid bit of campus slang. It never took him more than one stroke to behead the dummy dragon.

Gradually, his task was made more difficult. Paper gave way to papiermâché and finally to wood, but even the toughest of these dummy dragons had no terrors for Gawaine. One sweep of the ax always did the business. There were those who said that when the practice was protracted until dusk and the dragons threw long, fantastic shadows across the meadow, Gawaine did not charge so impetuously nor shout so loudly. But it is possible there was malice in this charge.

In any case, the headmaster decided by the end of June that it was time for the test. A dragon had come close to the school grounds only the night before and had eaten some of the lettuce from the garden. The faculty decided that Gawaine was ready. They gave him a diploma and a new battle-ax and the headmaster summoned him to a private conference.

"Sit down," said the headmaster. "Have a cigar."

Gawaine hesitated.

"Oh, I know it's against the rules," said the headmaster. "But after all, you have received your preliminary degree. You are no longer a boy. You are a man. Tomorrow you will go out into the world, the great world of achievement."

Gawaine took a cigar. The headmaster offered him a match, but he pro-duced one of his own and began to puff away with a dexterity that quite amazed the principal.

"Here you have learned the theories of life," continued the headmaster, resuming the thread of his discourse, "but after all, life is not a matter of theories. Life is a matter of facts. It calls on the young and the old alike to face these facts, even though they are hard and sometimes unpleasant. Your problem, for example, is to slay dragons."

"They say that those dragons down in the south wood are five hundred feet long," ventured Gawaine, timorously.

"Stuff and nonsense!" exclaimed the headmaster. "The curate saw one last week from the top of Arthur's Hill. The dragon was sunning himself down in the valley. The curate didn't have an opportunity to look at him very long because he felt it was his duty to hurry back to make a report to me. He said the monster—or shall I say, the big lizard—wasn't an inch over two hundred feet.

"But the size has nothing at all to do with it. You'll find the big ones even easier than the little ones. They're far slower on their feet and less aggressive, I'm told. Besides, before you go I'm going to equip you in such fashion that you need have no fear of all the dragons in the world."

"I'd like an enchanted cap," said Gawaine.

"What's that?" asked the headmaster, testily.

"A cap to make me disappear," explained Gawaine.

The headmaster laughed indulgently. "You mustn't believe all those old wives' stories," he said. "There isn't any such thing. A cap to make you disappear, indeed! What would you do with it? You haven't even appeared yet. Why, my boy, you could walk from here to London, and nobody would so much as look at you. You're nobody. You couldn't be more invis-ible than that."

Gawaine seemed dangerously close to a relapse into his old habit of whimpering. The headmaster reassured him: "Don't worry; I'll give you something much better than an enchanted cap. I'm going to give you a magic word. All you have to do is to repeat this magic charm once and no dragon can possibly harm a hair of your head. You can cut off his head at your leisure."

He took a heavy book from the shelf behind his desk and began to run through it. "Sometimes," he said, "the charm is a whole phrase or even a sentence. I might, for instance, give you 'To make the'—no, that might not do. I think a single word would be the best for dragons."

"A short word," suggested Gawaine.

"It can't be too short or it wouldn't be potent. There isn't so much hurry as all that. Here's a splendid magic word: 'Rumplesnitz.' Do you think you can learn that?"

Gawaine tried, and in an hour or so he seemed to have the word well in hand. Again and again he interrupted the lesson to inquire, "And if I say 'Rumplesnitz,' the dragon can't possibly hurt me?"

And always the headmaster replied, "If you only say "Rumplesnitz,' you are perfectly safe."

Toward morning Gawaine seemed resigned to his career. When daybreak came, the headmaster saw him to the edge of the forest and pointed out the direction in which he should proceed. About a mile away to the southwest, a cloud of steam hovered over an open meadow in the woods, and the head-master assured Gawaine that under the steam he would find a dragon. Gawaine went forward slowly. He wondered whether it would be best to ap-proach the dragon on the run, as he did in his practice in the south meadow, or to walk slowly toward him, shouting "Rumplesnitz" all the way.

The problem was decided for him. No sooner had he come to the fringe of the meadow than the dragon spied him and began to charge. It was a large dragon and yet it seemed decidedly aggressive in spite of the head-master's statement to the contrary. As the dragon charged, it released huge clouds of hissing steam through its nostrils. It was almost as if a gi-gantic teapot had gone mad.

The dragon came forward so fast and Gawaine was so frightened that he had time to say "Rumplesnitz" only once. As he said it, he swung his battle-ax and off popped the head of the dragon. Gawaine had to admit that it was even easier to kill a real dragon that a wooden one if only you said "Rumplesnitz."

Gawaine brought home the ears and a small section of the tail. His schoolmates and the faculty made much of him, but the headmaster wisely kept him from being spoiled by insisting that he go on with his work. Every clear day Gawaine rose at dawn and went out to kill dragons. The headmaster kept him at home when it rained, because he said the woods were damp and unhealthy at such times and he didn't want the boy to run needless risks.

Few good days passed in which Gawaine failed to get a dragon. On one particularly fortunate day, he killed three—a husband and wife and a vis-iting relative. Gradually he developed a technique.

Pupils who sometimes watched him from the hilltops a long way off said that he often allowed the dragon to come within a few feet before he said "Rumplesnitz." He came to say it with a mocking sneer. Occasionally he did stunts. Once, when an excursion party from London was watching him, he went into action with his right hand tied behind his back. The dragon's head came off just as easily.

As Gawaine's record of killings mounted higher, the headmaster found it impossible to keep him completely in hand. He fell into the habit of stealing out at night and engaging in long drinking bouts at the village tavern. It was after such a debauch that he rose a little before dawn one fine August morning and started out after his fiftieth dragon.

Gawaine's head was heavy and his mind sluggish. He was heavy in other respects as well, for he had adopted the somewhat vulgar practice of wearing his medals, ribbons and all, when he went out dragon hunting. The decorations began on his chest and ran all the way down to his abdomen. They must have weighed at least eight pounds.

Gawaine found a dragon in the same meadow where he had killed the first one. It was a fair-sized dragon, but evidently an old one. Its face was wrinkled and Gawaine thought he had never seen so hideous a countenance. Much to the lad's disgust, the monster refused to charge, and Gawaine was obliged to walk toward it. He whistled as he went. The dragon regarded him hopelessly, but craftily; of course it had heard of Gawaine. Even when the lad raised his battle-ax, the dragon made no move. It knew that there was no salvation in the quickest thrust of the head, for it had been informed that this hunter was protected by an enchantment. The dragon merely waited, hoping something would turn up.

Gawaine raised the battle-ax and suddenly lowered it again. He had grown very pale and he trembled violently. The dragon suspected a trick. "What's the matter?" it asked with false solicitude.

"I've forgotten the magic word," stammered Gawaine.

"What a pity," said the dragon. "So that was the secret. It doesn't seem quite sporting to me, all this magic stuff, you know. Not cricket, as we used to say when I was a little dragon; but after all, that's a matter of opinion."

Gawaine was so helpless with terror that the dragon's confidence rose immeasurably and it could not resist the temptation to show off a bit. "Could I possibly be of any assistance?" it asked. "What's the first letter of the magic word?"

"It begins with an 'r,' " Gawaine answered weakly.

"Let's see," mused the dragon, "that doesn't tell us much, does it? What sort of a word is this? Is it an epithet, do you think?" Gawaine could do no more than nod. "Why, of course," exclaimed the dragon, "reactionary Republican." Gawaine shook his head. "Well, then," it said, "we'd better get down to business. Will you surrender?"

With the suggestion of a compromise, Gawaine mustered up enough courage to speak. "What will you do if I surrender?" he asked.

"Why, I'll eat you," said the dragon.

"And if I don't surrender?"

"I'll eat you just the same."

"Then it doesn't make any difference, does it?" moaned Gawaine.

"It does to me," said the dragon with a smile. "I'd rather you didn't surrender. You'd taste much better if you didn't." The dragon waited a long time for Gawaine to ask why, but the boy was too frightened to speak. Finally, the dragon had to give the explanation without its cue. "You see," it said, "if you don't surrender you'll taste better because you'll die game."

This was an old and ancient trick of the dragon's. By means of some such quip he was accustomed to paralyze his victims with laughter and then destroy them. Gawaine was sufficiently paralyzed as it was, but laughter had no part in his helplessness. With the last word of the joke, the dragon drew back his head and struck. In that second, the magic word "Rumplesnitz" flashed into Gawaine's mind, but there was no time for him to say it. There was time only to strike and, without a word, Gawaine met the onrush of the dragon with a full swing. He put all his back and shoulders into it. The impact was terrific and the head of the dragon flew almost 100 yards and landed in a thicket.

Gawaine did not remain frightened for very long after the death of the dragon. His mood was one of wonder and enormous puzzlement. Almost in a trance, he cut off the ears of the monster. Again and again, he thought to himself, "I didn't say 'Rumplesnitz'!" He was sure of that, and yet there was no question that he had killed the dragon. In fact, he had never killed one so utterly. Never before had he driven a head for anything like the same distance; twenty-five yards was perhaps his best previous record. All the way back to the knight school, he kept rumbling about in his mind, seeking an explanation for what had occurred.

He went immediately to the headmaster, and after closing the door told him what had happened. "I didn't say 'Rumplesnitz,'" he explained with great earnestness.

The headmaster laughed. "I'm glad you've found out," he said. "It makes you ever so much more of a hero. Don't you see that? Now you know that it was you who killed all these dragons and not that foolish little word 'Rumplesnitz.'"

Gawaine frowned. "Then it wasn't a magic word after all?" he asked.

"Of course not," said the headmaster, "you ought to be too old for such foolishness. There isn't any such thing as a magic word."

"But you told me it was magic," protested Gawaine. "You said it was magic and now you say it isn't."

"It wasn't magic in a literal sense," answered the headmaster, "but it was much more wonderful than that. The word gave you confidence. It took away your fears. If I hadn't told you that, you might have been killed the very first time. It was your battle-ax did the trick."

Gawaine was obviously distressed by the explanation, and the headmaster was surprised by the boy's attitude. Interrupting a long philosophic and ethical discourse by the principal, Gawaine stammered, "If I hadn't of hit 'em all mighty hard and fast any one of 'em might have crushed me like a, like a ... " He fumbled for a word.

"Egg shell," suggested the headmaster.

"Like an egg shell," assented Gawaine, and he said it many times. All through the evening meal, people within earshot heard him muttering, "Like an egg shell, like an egg shell."

The next day was clear, but Gawaine did not get up at dawn. Indeed, it was almost noon when the headmaster found him cowering in bed, with the clothes pulled over his head. The principal called the assistant professor of Pleasaunce and together they dragged the boy toward the forest.

"He'll be all right as soon as he gets a couple more dragons under his belt," explained the headmaster.

The assistant professor agreed. "It would be a shame to stop such a fine run," he said. "Why, counting that one yesterday, he's killed fifty dragons."

They pushed the boy into a thicket, above which hung a meager cloud of steam. It was obviously quite a small dragon. But Gawaine did not come back that night or the next. In fact, he never returned. Some weeks afterward, brave spirits from the school explored the thicket, but all they could find of Gawaine were the metal parts of his medals. Even the ribbons had been devoured.

The headmaster and assistant professor agreed that it would be better not to tell the school how Gawaine had achieved his record and especially not how he came to die. They held that it might have a bad effect on school spirit. Accordingly, Gawaine has lived in the memory of the school as its greatest hero. No visitor succeeds in leaving the building today without seeing a great shield that hangs on the wall of the dining hall. Fifty pairs of dragons' ears are mounted upon the shield and underneath in gilt letters is "Gawaine Le Coeur-Hardy," followed by the simple inscription, "He killed fifty dragons." The record has never been equaled.

Note: "The Fifty-First Dragon" was originally published in the collection, *Modern Essays*, edited by Christopher Morley (Harcourt Brace, 1921).

Seizing the Nettles
(Scotland)

Once upon a time, a wee lad was walking through the forest and came upon a patch of nettles. Fascinated by the unusual clusters, he tried to pluck the nettles and take them home to show his mama. But the plant stung him painfully and he raced home, his fingers stinging. "I scarcely touched it mama!" the lad cried.

"That is exactly why it stung you," his mama replied. "The next time you touch a nettle, grab it boldly, and it will be soft as silk in your hand and not hurt you in the least. Don't hesitate. Grab things boldly. If you are undecided, things may sting you. If you don't do things with all your might, you may end up being harmed by those things you try hesitantly."

Thoughts About the Stories, Discussions, and Activities

THE HUMMINGBIRD

In this tale, we see how one of nature's smallest creatures has a big belief that it too can help.

- *Have you ever been told that you're "just a kid" or "too young to help out"? Make a list of activities from which you've been excluded and brainstorm ways that you could get involved.*

THE FIFTY-FIRST DRAGON

This is a creative look at what gives us confidence, and how we develop or don't develop it.

- *What gives you confidence—compliments, achievements? What diminishes your confidence—put-downs, failures? Discuss how you can build your own self-confidence.*
- *Are there situations in which self-confidence can work against you? What are some of these? What is the difference between self-confidence and false pride?*
- *In this story, what token was given to the dragon slayer that he thought made him victorious? Identify and list any other such ideas or things that people still use in a superstitious manner to bring them "good luck" or self-confidence. Did*

your list include a rabbit's foot? Ask others if they have such an object, and share your findings. Discuss whether such superstitions are harmless or serve any positive purpose.

⊙ *Many professional athletes perform superstitious rituals before games. Gather newspaper articles that refer to this practice. How are these beliefs similar to the knight in "The Fifty-First Dragon"? Do these practices work?*

SEIZING THE NETTLES

This tale demonstrates how confidence can conquer the everyday problems we experience.

⊙ *What are nettles? See what you can find out about them by doing library and Internet research, then write a report.*

Other Activity Ideas

⊙ Educational researchers state that smaller classes give more advantages to the students, one of which is the value of self-confidence. Do you agree? Can you list reasons why this might be true? Interview students from smaller or larger classes about self-confidence. What questions might you ask them? Share your conclusions with others.

⊙ A teacher from New York instigated a project to build self-confidence in those around her. She honored her high school seniors by telling each of them the difference they made to her and the class. She then presented each with a blue ribbon that read in gold letters, "Who I Am Makes a Difference." They were then instructed to go out and honor others.

  ⊙ Can you predict what followed? Tell or write stories that you imagine might have come from this idea.
  ⊙ Did your stories involve people of power, youngsters, those in desperate straits, the hard-to-love, or the neglected?
  ⊙ Decorate cards to distribute with the statement "Who You Are Makes a Difference" on them. Follow up, if possible, on any results of this action.

⊙ Find a copy of the book Carrot Seed by Ruth Krauss, illustrated by Crockett Johnson (New York: Scholastic, 1945), in your school or public library. Read and study it for its implications regarding self-confidence. Share it with others and *discuss its values. Can a picture book instill the ideas of self-confidence in its readers/listeners?*

⊙ *Prepare a list of activities that you have never or rarely done before (e.g., recite a poem, tell a joke, sing a song, read aloud an essay). Pick one of these activities; first rehearse it with a friend, then with a small group, a larger group, or an even larger group. After each performance, applaud with the whole group. How does this experience affect self-confidence?*

See the "General Activities" section at the back of this book for ideas to further explore these topics.

Compassion

The Badger's Money
(Japan)

It is a common saying among men that to forget favors received is not the part of a bird or a beast. An ungrateful man will be ill spoken of by all the world. And yet, even birds and beasts will show gratitude. A man who does not repay a favor is worse even than dumb brutes. Is this not a disgrace?

Once upon a time, in a hut at a place called Namekata, in Hitachi, there lived an old priest famous neither for learning nor wisdom, but bent only on passing his days in prayer and meditation. He had not even a child to wait upon him, but prepared his food with his own hands. Night and morning he recited the Buddhist prayer "Namu Amida Butsu," which means "Save us eternal Buddha." He was intent on that alone.

Although the fame of his virtue did not reach far, his neighbors respected and revered him and often brought him food and raiment. When his roof or his walls fell out of repair, they would mend them for him, and so for the things of this world he took no thought.

One very cold night, when he thought no one was outside, he heard a voice calling, "Your reverence! Your reverence!" When he rose and went out to see who it was, there he beheld an old badger. Any ordinary man would have been greatly alarmed at this standing beast, but the priest, being such as he was, showed no sign of fear. "What is your business?" he asked the badger.

The badger respectfully bent its knees and replied, "My lair has been in the mountains. Snow or frost do not bother me, but now I am growing old and this severe cold is more than I can bear. I pray you let me enter and warm myself at the fire in your cottage so that I may live through this bitter night."

When the priest heard what a helpless state the beast was reduced to, he was filled with pity and said, "That's a very slight matter. Make haste and come in and warm yourself." Delighted with such a good reception, the badger went into the hut and squatted down by the fire to warm itself. The priest, with renewed fervor, recited his prayer and struck his bell before the image of Buddha, looking straight before him the whole time.

After two hours, the badger left with profuse expressions of thanks. From that time forth, it came every night to the hut, bringing with it dried branches and dead leaves it had collected for firewood. The priest at last got used to its company and, in fact, became very friendly with it. Whenever the badger did not arrive, the priest missed it and wondered why it did not come.

When the springtime came at the end of the second month, the badger gave up its visits. However, when winter returned, the beast resumed its old habit of coming to the hut. After this practice had gone on for ten years, one day the badger said to the priest, "Through your kindness for all these years I have been able to pass the winter nights in comfort. Your favors are such that during all my life, and even after my death, I must remember them. What can I do to repay you for your kindness? Is there anything that you wish for? Tell me."

The priest smiled at this speech and answered, "Being such as I am, I have no desire and no wishes. Glad as I am to hear your kind intentions, there is nothing that I can ask you to do for me. You need feel no anxiety on my account. As long as I live, when the winter comes, you shall be welcome here."

On hearing this, the badger could not conceal its admiration for the depth of the old man's benevolence. However, with so much to be grateful for, the badger felt hurt at not being able to repay the old man's kindness.

This was a subject that the badger often brought up, and the priest finally, touched by the goodness of the badger's heart said, "Since I have shaven my head, renounced the world, and forsaken the pleasures of this life, I have no desire to gratify. Yet, I would like to possess three riyos in gold. Food and clothes I receive by the favor of the villagers so take no heed for those things. Were I to die tomorrow and attain my wish of being born again into the next world, the same kind folk have promised to meet and bury my body.

"Therefore, although I have no other reason to wish for money, still if I had three riyos I would offer them up at some holy shrine so that masses and prayers might be said for me. Those prayers might help me enter into salvation. I would not get this money by violent or unlawful means. I only think of what might be if I had it. So you see, since you have expressed such kind feelings toward me, I have told you what is on my mind."

When the priest had finished speaking, the badger leaned its head to one side with a puzzled and anxious look. This made the old man very sorry that he had expressed a wish that seemed to give the beast trouble. He tried to take back his request, "Posthumous honors, after all, are the wish of ordinary men. I, who am a priest, ought not to entertain such thoughts or to want money. I pray that you pay no attention to what I have said."

Pretending to agree with what the priest had impressed upon it, the badger returned to the hills as usual. However, from that time forth, the badger did not come to the hut. The priest thought that this was very strange, but imagined that either the badger stayed away because it did not like to come without the money or that it had been killed during an attempt to steal it. He blamed himself for having added to his sins for no purpose, and even though it appeared to be too late, he repented. Since he felt the badger must have been killed, he passed his time in putting up prayers upon prayers for it.

Three years had gone by, when one night the old man heard a voice near his door calling out, "Your reverence! Your reverence!" It sounded like the badger, so he jumped up as soon as he heard it and ran to open the door. There, sure enough, was the badger. The priest in great delight, cried out, "And so you are safe and sound after all! Why have you been gone so long without coming here? I have been expecting and hoping for you anxiously for a long while."

The badger came into the hut and said, "If the money which you want had been for unlawful purposes, I could easily have gotten it. In fact, I could have gotten as much as you might have wanted. When I heard that it was to be offered to a temple for masses for your soul, I thought that if I were to steal the hidden treasure of some other man, you could not apply the money to a sacred purpose. So I went to the island of Sado, an island on the west coast of Japan famous for its gold mines, and gathered the sand and earth, which had been cast away as worthless by the miners. I melted it in the fire and at this work I spent months and days."

As the badger finished speaking, the priest looked at the money that it had produced, and sure enough, he saw that it was bright and new and clean. He took the money and raised it respectfully to his head. "You have had all this toil and labor on account of a foolish speech of mine? I have obtained my heart's desire and I am truly grateful."

As he was thanking the badger with great politeness and ceremony, the beast said, "In doing this I have fulfilled my own wish. Still I hope that you will not tell what has happened to any man."

"Indeed," replied the priest. "I cannot choose but tell this story. For if I keep this money in my poor hut, it will be stolen by thieves. I must either give it to someone to keep for me, or else at once offer it up at the temple. When I do this, when people see a poor old priest with such a large amount of money, quite unfit to his station in life, they will think it very suspicious. I will have to tell the story of how I came to have it. I will say that the badger that gave me the money has ceased coming to my hut. That way you will not fear being waylaid. You will be able to come as of old and take shelter from the cold."

The badger agreed to this. As long as the old priest lived, the badger came and spent the winter nights with him. Respect and gratitude was part of their lives together.

Arion and His Harp
(Greece)

In the court of Periander, king of Corinth, dwelt Arion, the greatest singer of tales. Arion was a special favorite of the king.

"There is to be a musical contest in Sicily and I want to compete for the prize," Arion told Periander.

"Stay with me. Be contented," advised the king. "He who strives to win in contests of all kinds may lose. Besides, I want you to stay here with me."

"A wandering life is happiness for a bard. I want to share my talents and joys with others," said Arion. "Besides, if I win the prize, my fame will be increased along with my pleasure at winning."

So Arion left Corinth for Sicily, where he became undisputed winner of the contest. After a day of celebration, he boarded a Corinthian ship with his chest full of newly won riches and reward. He was eager to return to Corinth and share his victory and riches with his friend, King Periander.

The waters were calm, the breezes gentle, and the sky cloudless. It wasn't the travel that would prove hazardous; danger came from the greed of men. Arion had taken a stroll on the deck, and he overheard the seamen plotting to kill him for his riches. There was nowhere to go to escape. When the crew approached him, they yelled, "Arion, you must die! If you want to be buried onshore, surrender to us and die on this spot. Otherwise, throw yourself into the sea."

"Take my gold if that is what you want, but spare my life," Arion pleaded.

"No! You must die. Alive you would tell Periander, and we would never be able to escape from him. You must die!" they decreed.

"Then you must grant me one last wish," he asked. "If I must die, I would like to die as I have lived, as a bard with my death song and my harp strings winging their way in the breezes. Then I will bid farewell to life and go to my fate."

Even the rude and crude admire beauty, and these pirates were eager to hear such a famous musician, so they agreed.

"I must dress in proper clothes for such a performance," Arion said. "Apollo would be disappointed to meet me unless I was clad in my minstrel raiments." He dressed himself in a gold and purple tunic with graceful billows, his jewels on his arms, a golden wreath on his fair head, and exquisite perfume. He held his lyre in his left hand and struck it with an ivory wand. Arion appeared to be inspired as he smelled the morning air and admired the glittering morning rays.

The seamen were entranced as Arion went to stand on the side of the vessel. He looked down into the deep blue sea and began to sing of his new life among the gods and wise ones. As the last notes of his harp strings vibrated in the air, he turned and leapt off the boat. His tunic floated like wings in the air. He soon was covered by the waves and gone from sight.

The evil crew felt safe and continued on their way to Corinth, feeling secure that their crime would not be detected.

What the crewmen did not know, however, was that Arion's music had enchanted the inhabitants of the deep to come closer to listen, and that dolphins had followed the ship as if chained by a spell. As Arion started to float toward the surface of the water, a dolphin offered him his back out of compassion. Arion mounted the dolphin, which carried him safely to shore.

At the spot on the rocky shore where Arion landed, there was later erected a monument of brass to preserve the memory of this amazing event.

After bidding farewell to the dolphin, Arion started his trip on foot to Corinth. He played and sang as he went, quite full of love and happiness. When he entered the halls of Periander, he was grateful for what he had—life and music. When he told Periander what had happened, the king ordered him to stay hidden so that when the evildoers came to report on their arrival, they would not know that Arion had been saved.

When the ship arrived in the harbor, Periander summoned the mariners before him. "Have you heard anything of my beloved friend Arion?" he asked them. "I am quite anxious for his return."

"We left him well and prosperous in Tarentum," they said. Just as they spoke, Arion stepped forth and faced them. The criminals fell prostrate at his feet and cried, "We meant to kill you, but you have returned as a god."

"He lives," said Periander. "He lives, the master of music. Kind heaven protects men such as him. You greedy murderers are lucky that Arion does not seek revenge. Be gone with you all. May your lives never experience the sights and sounds of beauty again."

Arion lived many more years to create celestial music and sing the praises of the compassionate dolphins.

The Grateful Foxes
(Japan)

One fine spring day, two friends went out to a moor to gather
fern, attended by a boy with a bottle of wine and a box of
provisions. As they were wandering about, they saw at the foot of
a hill two foxes that had brought out their cubs to play. The
friends looked on, struck by the strangeness of what they saw
next—three children had come up from a neighboring village
with baskets in their hands.

As soon as the children saw the foxes, they picked up a bamboo stick and stealthily followed the creatures in the rear. The
old foxes took flight, and the children seized the cubs, surrounded them, and beat them with the stick. When all but one
of the cubs ran off, two of the boys held down the remaining fox
and seized it by the scruff of its neck. They went off in high glee.

The two friends were looking on the whole time, and one of
them shouted out, "Hallo! You boys! What are you doing with
that fox?"

The oldest of the boys replied, "We are going to take him
home and sell him to a young man in our village. He will buy
him and then he'll boil him in a pot and eat him!"

"Well," replied the fellow, after considering the matter attentively, "I suppose it's all the same to you whom you sell him to.
You'd better let me have him."

"Oh, but the young man from our village promised us a good
sum if we could find a fox. He got us to come out to the hills and
catch one. We can't sell him to you at any price."

"Well, I suppose it cannot be helped then. How much would the young man give you for the cub?"

"Oh, he'll give us three hundred cash at least," the boy answered.

"I'll give you that and half more," said the fellow. "You'll gain cash by the transaction."

"Oh, we'll sell him for that, sir. How shall we hand him over to you?" he asked.

"Just tie him up here," said the fellow. The boy tied the cub around the neck with the string of the napkin in which the lunch box was wrapped.

The man gave the boys the money and they ran away delighted.

The man's friend said, "Well, certainly you have got queer tastes. What on earth are you going to keep the fox for?"

"How very unkind of you to speak of my tastes like that. If we had not interfered just now, the fox's cub would have lost its life. If we had not seen the affair, there would have been no help for it. How could I stand by and see life taken? It was but a little I spent to save the cub, but had it cost a fortune I should not have grudged it. I thought you knew me well enough to know my heart. Today you have accused me of being eccentric and I see how mistaken I have been in you. Our friendship shall cease from this day forth."

He said this with a great deal of firmness. The other bowed with his hands on his knees as he stepped backwards, "Indeed, indeed. I am filled with admiration at the goodness of your heart. When I hear you speak in this way I feel more than ever how great is the respect I have for you. I thought that you just might wish to use the cub as a sort of decoy to lead the old ones to you so you could pray to them to bring you prosperity and virtue. When I called you eccentric just now, I was just trying your heart. I am truly ashamed of myself."

As he spoke, still bowing, the other replied, "Really! Was that indeed your thought? Then I pray you to forgive me for my violent language."

The two friends had reconciled. They examined the cub and saw that its foot was slightly wounded and it could not walk. While they were thinking what they should do, they spied out the herb called "Doctor's Nakase," which was just sprouting. They rolled up a little of it in their fingers and applied it to the wound. Then they pulled out some boiled rice from their luncheon box and offered it to the cub, but it showed no sign of wanting to eat. They stroked it gently on its back and petted it.

The pain of the wound seemed to have subsided. The two friends were admiring the healing properties of the herb, when they noticed the old foxes sitting and watching them by the side of some stacks of rice straw.

"Look there! The old foxes have come back out of fear for their cub's safety. Come, we will set it free!" With these words, they untied the string from the cub's neck and turned its head toward the spot where the old foxes sat. The wounded foot was no longer painful and with one bound the cub dashed to its parents' side. The cub licked them all over for joy. The old foxes seemed to bow their thanks looking at the two friends.

The two men, with peace in their hearts, went off to another place. They found a pretty spot, got out the bottle of wine and ate their noonday meal. After a pleasant day, they returned to their homes and became firmer friends than ever.

The man who had rescued the fox cub was a pretty well off tradesman. He had three or four agents and two maidservants, besides men servants. Altogether, they lived pretty nicely. He was married, and he and his wife had one son who had just celebrated his tenth birthday.

Shortly after his birthday, the boy developed a strange disease that defied all the skill and drugs of the physicians. At last, a famous physician prescribed the liver taken from a live fox. "This will certainly effect a cure," he said.

When the parents heard this, they were at their wit's end. They told a man who lived on the mountains what the physician had prescribed. "Even though our child should die for it," they said, "we will not ourselves deprive another creature of its life. You who live among the hills are sure to hear when your neighbors go out fox hunting. We don't care what price we have to pay for a fox's liver. Buy one for us at any expense." The man of the mountain promised to execute the commission and went on his way.

The following night there came a messenger. "I have come from the man of the mountain. His messenger awaits you." So, the master of the house went out to see him.

"I have just come with news that last night, the fox's liver that you required fell into a hunter's hands. He sent me to bring it to you." With these words, the messenger produced a small jar, adding, "In a few days he will let you know the price."

After he had heard this message, the master of the house was greatly pleased and said. "I am indeed deeply grateful for this kindness. It will save my son's life."

Then the sick boy's mother came out and received the jar with every mark of politeness. "We must make a present to the messenger," she said.

His reply was, "Indeed sir, I have already been paid for my trouble."

"Well at any rate, you must stop the night here," replied the father.

"Thank you, sir. I have a relation in the next village whom I have not seen for a long while. I will pass the night with him." So, the messenger took his leave.

The parents lost no time in sending news to the physician that they had procured the fox's liver. The next day, the doctor came and compounded a medicine for the boy, which at once produced a good effect. There was great joy in the household. As luck would have it, three days after this, the man of the mountain came to their house. They hurried out to meet and welcome him.

"How quickly you fulfilled our wishes. How kind of you to send it at once! The doctor prepared the medicine and now our boy can get up and walk about the room. It's is all due to your goodness."

"Wait a bit!" cried the guest, who did not know what to make of this news from the two parents. "I found it impossible to get a fox's liver for you, so I came today to make my excuses. Now I really can't understand what you are so grateful to me for."

"We are thanking you, sir," replied the master of the house, bowing with his hands on the ground, "for the fox's liver that we asked you to obtain for us."

"I really am perfectly unaware of having sent you a fox's liver. There must be some mistake here. Please investigate the matter carefully," he told them.

"Well, this is very strange," said the father, "Four nights ago, a man of some five or six and thirty years of age came with a verbal message from you to the effect that you had sent him with a fox's liver. He told us you had just received it and said that he would come and tell us the price another day. When we asked him to spend the night here, he answered that he would lodge with a relation in the next village and then he left."

The visitor was more and more lost in amazement. Leaning his head to one side in deep thought, he confessed that he could make no sense of it. As for the husband and wife, they felt quite disturbed that they had thanked a man so warmly for favors of which he denied all knowledge. The visitor took his leave and went back to the mountain.

That night there appeared at the pillow of the master of the house, a woman of about one or two and thirty years of age. She said, "I am the fox that lives near the mountain. Last spring when I was taking my cubs out to play, one was carried off by some boys. It was only saved by your goodness. Your problems pierced me to my heart. I thought I might be of use to you. Your son's illness could not be cured without a liver taken from a live fox, so to repay your kindness, I killed my cub. I took outs its liver. My husband disguised himself as a messenger and brought it to your house."

As she spoke, the fox shed tears. The master of the house, wishing to thank her, moved in bed. His wife awoke and asked him what was the matter. To her great astonishment, she saw he was biting the pillow and weeping bitterly. "Why are you weeping?" she asked.

At last, he sat up in bed and told her, "Last spring when I was out on a pleasure excursion, I saved the life of a fox's cub. The other day I told the man of the mountain that, although my son would die before my eyes, I would not be able to kill a fox on purpose. I asked him, in case he heard of any hunter killing a fox, to buy it for me.

"How the foxes came to hear of this I do not know. The foxes to whom I had shown kindness killed their own cub and took out its liver. The old dog-fox, disguising himself as a messenger from the man of the mountain, came here with it. His mate has just been at my pillow side and told me all about it. That is why I was moved to tears."

When she heard this, his wife likewise was blinded by her tears. For a while they lay lost in thought, but at last came to themselves. They lighted the lamp on the shelf and spent the night reciting prayers and praises. The next day, they told what had happened to their household, relatives, and friends. There had never been an example of foxes killing their own cubs to help another. The story became the talk of the whole countryside.

The boy who had recovered through the medicine selected the prettiest spot on their land to erect a shrine to the fox god, and offered sacrifice to the two old foxes. The family always remembered the great gift the foxes had given to them.

Note: Reprinted from *Story Medicine: Multicultural Tales of Healing and Transformation* by Norma J. Livo ©2001 Libraries Unlimited.

The Fox and the Horse
(Germany, Brothers Grimm)

A peasant once had a faithful horse that had grown old and could do no more work, so his master would no longer give him anything to eat and said, "I can certainly make no more use of you, but still I mean well by you. If you prove yourself still strong enough to bring me a lion here, I will maintain you. Now take yourself away out of my stable." With that, he chased the horse into the open country. The horse was angry, and went to the forest to seek a little protection from the weather.

There, he met a fox, who asked, "Why do you hang your head so, and go about all alone?"

"Alas," replied the horse, "avarice and fidelity do not dwell together in one house. My master has forgotten what services I have performed for him for so many years, and because I can no longer plough well, he will give me no more food, and has driven me out."

"Without giving you a chance?" asked the fox.

"The chance was a bad one," answered the horse. "He said if I were still strong enough to bring him a lion, he would keep me, but he well knows that I cannot do that."

The fox said, "I will help you. Just lay yourself down, stretch yourself out, as if you were dead, and do not stir." The horse did as the fox instructed, and the fox went to the lion, which had his den not far off. "A dead horse is lying outside there," he said to the lion. "Just come with me and you can have a rich meal."

The lion went with him, and when they were both standing by the horse, the fox said, "After all, it is not very comfortable for you here—I tell you what—I will fasten it to you by the tail, and then you can drag the horse into your cave and devour it in peace." This advice pleased the lion, and he lay down quietly so that the fox could tie the horse fast to him. But the fox tied the lion's legs together with the horse's tail, and twisted and fastened all so well and so strongly that no amount of flailing could break it.

When he had finished his work, he tapped the horse on the shoulder and said, "Pull, white horse, pull." At once the horse sprang up and hauled the lion away with him. The lion began to roar so that all the birds in the forest flew out in terror, but the horse let him roar. He drew and dragged the lion over the country to his master's door.

When the master saw the lion, he was of a better mind and said to the horse, "You shall stay here with me and fare well." Thereafter, the farmer gave the horse plenty to eat until he died.

The Golden Lion
(Italy)

A very rich merchant had three sons. His wife had died and left him to raise their sons alone. He had been a good father and did the best he could to show and teach them how to become good men.

The oldest son was a bit arrogant, but that was just a result of being shown such deference as the son of a rich merchant. The second son was proud and of goodwill; he seemed to live in the shadow of his oldest brother. The youngest son was humble and full of compassion. He cared for wounded birds and animals, and helped people when he saw their need. This son was happy and contented with life.

Eventually, the oldest son became restless and desired to see more of the world and learn about other cultures. "Father, I would like to travel and meet new people and learn new things. Would you provide me with a ship equipped to travel and find adventure?"

After much thought, his father decided that this would be a proper education for his son and heir. Hadn't he himself profited from observing how people were the same yet different? Hadn't that information helped make him a wealthy merchant? "Yes, son," he replied, "you are right. It is time you learned how to cope with others and solve problems as you come across them. I will have a fine ship outfitted for you."

After some weeks, the young man sailed away in his proud ship with banners fluttering in the breezes. How he looked forward to this chance to travel and learn. Again, weeks passed, and his ship was blown into a large seaside city. Venturing ashore and throughout the city, he saw notices in which the king there proclaimed, "If any man can find my daughter, he will have her as his wife. If he tries and fails to find her, his head will be the forfeit."

"Well," thought the oldest son, "this is adventure, just as I sought it. That should not be such a difficult task." He made his way to the king and told him, "I have seen your notices throughout the city and I wish to seek the princess."

"Ah! Are you brave and eager for this?" asked the king. "If so, here are the rules. You will have eight days to search her out. You will have the whole palace to search in. If you find her, there will be a royal wedding. If you don't find her, there will be a royal execution."

With that, the king ordered the doors to be thrown open to the castle. He commanded that food and drink be brought to the young man. The merchant's oldest son ate his fill and then began his search for the princess. He was amazed at all the possible hiding places in the castle. He searched every corner, every chamber, and every piece of furniture, but was not able to find her. And so, he searched for eight days.

"You have failed," pronounced the king, and had the young man taken to the courtyard, where his head was cut off.

During this time, the merchant and his two younger sons heard nothing from the eldest, and no incoming boats had news of him. They became anxious as to his travels, and finally the second son could stand it no longer. He went in to his father and declared, "Father! I fear something has happened to my brother. Provide me with a ship and money and goods to trade and let me go seek out my brother."

His father stroked his gray beard and looked at his son from his piercing eyes. "Son, I fear that trouble has come to my eldest. I would not have you also in danger."

"But father, I see your grief over my brother and I would go and find out news of him," begged the second son.

After some heated discussion, the father agreed. Again, he had a grand ship outfitted for his son and placed treasures on board for him to use in trade and barter. The son sailed away, with colored banners unfurled. Just as had happened to his older brother, winds drove him to the same seashore city, and he saw his brother's ship at anchor in the harbor.

"Ah, I know I follow in my brother's footsteps. I will see what I can find out about him," the second son thought. But no one knew the whereabouts of his brother. As he toured the city, the sights and sounds fascinated him, but he also saw the posted notices about finding the princess.

He decided to go to the palace and tell the king that he would like to take up this challenge.

"Do you realize the rules of this quest?" asked the king.

"Maybe you should tell me of them," requested the second son.

And so, the king again repeated the conditions of the search, "You will have eight days to find the princess. The palace will be open to you to pursue your goal. If you fail, you will, like many others before you, lose your head."

The second son felt that his oldest brother had probably been one of the many to lose their heads. "I will undertake this task. It cannot be too difficult of a matter," he told one of his men. Eight days later, he had fared no better than his brother and lost his head.

The merchant and his youngest son again heard no news of the second son and his efforts. They feared the worst. The merchant became melancholy and couldn't eat for worry about his sons. The youngest son felt great concern for his brothers and now for his father and his health. "Dear father, let me go and see if I can find my brothers. I worry for your wellbeing and I suffer the absence and lack of news of my brothers," pleaded the youngest.

"Ah son, I could not bear to lose you also," whispered a weary merchant. "If your brothers are lost to us, how could I survive your loss too?"

"I understand, father, but if there is anything I can do to find my brothers and relieve your mind, I must attempt it. Let me go, father," the youngest son reasoned.

After much discussion and pleading, the merchant could no longer refuse his son's request. "Go son, and be aware of all the dangers before you. Whatever you do, you are more precious to me than you can possibly understand. I must not lose you."

The ship equipped for the youngest son was the best vessel that had ever been built. Banners and flags flew proudly as the ship with the youngest son sailed from his home port. The trip was uneventful until again, the winds took control of the ship and blew it into the seaside city harbor where the youngest son saw the two ships of his brothers.

"I must search out any news of them," he told his captain. "Send the men throughout the city to discover any possible reason for their absence."

The crew spread throughout the city seeking news, but all they could come up with was the often-repeated comment, "If there are any young men missing, they may be among those seeking to find the princess, failing and are beheaded."

When this news reached the youngest son, he felt that if he were to find anything that might comfort his father, he must enter the search for the princess. On the road to the castle, he met an old woman who stopped him and begged, "Ah, young man. Please do not send me away empty handed. Surely you will not refuse an old woman a few pennies."

The young man felt sorry for the old woman and gave her some coins. "I see you are troubled," she told him after he had given her the money. "Tell me what it is and perhaps I will be able to help you out." He told her of his lost brothers and how he feared they had died.

"I would find the princess and end the deaths of young men who fail in their search," the young man said.

"I can easily help you with that," she answered. "The only problem is that you must have great amounts of gold."

"Oh, I have plenty. My father filled my ship with gold to help me in my mission. There is gold aplenty!" he declared.

"Well then, young man, you must take that gold to a goldsmith and have him make you a golden lion with eyes of crystal. Inside the lion, there must be something that will enable it to play tunes. When all is ready, bring it to me here," she instructed him.

The young man did as he was told. When the golden lion was before the old woman, she hid the youth in it and told his men to take it to the king. "I will come along with you and bring it to the king. He will be enchanted with it and want to buy it." And so it was done. The golden lion delighted the king and he wanted to buy it. "Dear king," the old woman told him, "It does not belong to me. I know that my master will not want to part with it for any price."

The king coveted the lion. "At any rate, leave it with me for a few days. I would like to show it to my daughter."

The old woman scratched her head and finally said, "Yes, I can do that. Tomorrow I must have it back again." The king agreed and the old woman went away.

The king watched her go until she was long out of sight. "I want to make sure that she will not spy on me," he told his followers. When he was sure that it would be safe, he had the golden lion carried to his room. He lifted some loose boards from the floor and opened the trapdoor to a staircase that went down to a door below it. The king unlocked the door and entered a narrow passage that was closed by another door, which he also opened.

Meanwhile, the young man, hidden in the golden lion, kept count of everything, and tallied up that there were seven doors in all. After these had all been unlocked, the king entered an elegantly furnished hall filled with dancing candles. The princess and eleven of her friends were cavorting in this grand hall. All twelve girls were dressed the same and looked like each other; in fact, it could be said that they looked like twelve peas in a pod.

The young man observed this fact and thought, "What bad luck this is. Even if I can manage to find my way here again, how would I ever be able to tell which girl was the princess?"

He kept watching carefully. The princess clapped her hands with joy and ran up to her father. "Oh, do let us keep that splendid beast for tonight. It will make such a unique plaything."

The king did not stay long and he was not able to deny the princess her wish. He loved her so dearly and wanted her to wed only the brightest, bravest, best young man in the whole world. He handed the lion to the girls, who played with it and danced around it until they grew sleepy. When it was time to go to bed, the princess took the lion to her own chamber. Just as she was beginning to doze off to sleep, she was startled by a voice quite close to her. "Oh lovely princess! If you only knew what I have gone through to find you!"

The princess jumped out of bed screaming, "The lion! The lion!" Her friends thought she was just having a nightmare and they did not trouble themselves to even get up.

"Oh lovely princess," continued the voice. "Fear nothing! I am the son of a rich merchant and desire above all things in the world to have you for my wife. In order to accomplish this, I hid myself in this golden lion."

"What use will that be to you?" she asked. "If you cannot pick me out from among my companions you will stand to lose your head."

"Therefore, I look to you to help me," he replied. "I have done so much to find you that you might do this one thing for me."

The princess thought for a moment. "Listen to me. On the eighth day, I shall tie a white sash around my waist. You will know me by that white sash."

The next morning, the king came early to fetch the lion. The old woman was at the palace asking for its return. When she had the lion safe from view, she let the young man out. Immediately, the merchant's youngest son went to the king. "I want to search for the princess," he told the king.

The king was almost tired of repeating the same words, but he did. "Very well. You have eight days to find the princess. The palace will be open to you to search for her. If you fail, you will lose your head, as have many young men before you. I want only the best, bravest, and brightest young man in the whole world to be her husband."

The young man thought of his father. "We will never see my brothers again, but this will end brutal deaths of others who seek her. That at least will be something positive. Also, I find her delightful and know you would too, father."

For seven days the young man roamed the castle, ate, enjoyed all the beautiful things around him, and pretended to search rooms, closets, corners, and furniture for the princess. On the eighth day, he entered the king's room.

"Take up the floor here," he ordered the surprised king.

The king gave a cry, but then demanded, "Why do you want the floor taken up? What do you think might be hidden there?"

The king and all of his courtiers looked at the young man, but he repeated, "Take up the floor here."

The young man went straight down the staircase until he reached the first door. He turned and demanded the key. The king was forced to unlock this door, and the next, and the next, and the next until all of the doors had been opened. They entered the hall where the twelve maidens stood in a row. They looked so alike the king felt sure that no one could tell them apart.

The princess looked at the young man, her eyes gleamed, and she slipped a white sash from her pocket to her waist. At that moment, the merchant's youngest son dashed to her and claimed, "This is the princess. I claim her for my wife."

The king had to admit defeat, and commanded that the wedding feast should be prepared.

After eight days, the bridal pair said farewell to the king, who provided a dowry of treasures for the princess, and they set sail for the young man's home country. The merchant's youngest son had not forgotten the old woman, and before they left, he gifted her with the golden lion. With that, she would live in comfort until the end of her days.

The Deer of India
(India)

Once, a long time ago in far-off India, there lived a king. He had power over all, and was used to having his commands carried out. In the forests near the king lived a herd of Banyan deer, with eyes that were the color of gold, horns as white as silver, and mouths like bright red flowers. With large bodies and fine tails, their hooves were bright and hard as they pranced in the forest.

Despite the king's constant hunting, the deer thrived in the forest. There were 500 Banyan deer, including the king of their herd. Also in the nearby forest, lived a herd known as Monkey deer, which was led by its own king deer.

The king of the people was in the habit of regularly hunting the deer with bows and arrows. That was because his favorite food was deer meat. Some people like to eat sweets, some prefer fish, but the king desired deer meat. He didn't like to go hunting alone, so he asked people from his village to join him. The king and his people went hunting day after day.

The townspeople grumbled over this, though, because although they did enjoy hunting, they weren't left with enough time to get their work done. Some of the grumblers got together to devise a plan to spend more of their time at their regular work and less of it hunting. They brainstormed all sorts of ideas on how to accomplish this, but they finally decided the best plan was to make a park that they could drive the deer into.

They felt that with the deer driven into a park, the king could go there and hunt, while they could get on with their daily work. And so it was that they built the park, provided for its source of water, planted grass, and built a fence around it.

When it was finished, they closed the gate to the park and went to tell the king that his hunting would now be closer and not require villagers to go with him every day. They led the king to the park to introduce him to it, but he was struck with the appearance of the two deer kings. He was so impressed with their regal presence that he declared, "From this day forth, no one will hunt you. You will not be killed, but your lives will be spared so you can rule over your herds."

The king was also impressed with the great herds. It was so much easier to see them now that they were in an open park and no longer in the forest. The king went to the park to hunt deer, but instead of having villagers help him with the hunting, he took his cook with him.

The deer began to recognize what happened when the king and his cook came to the park. They saw other deer drop dead when they were shot with the arrows. Soon, the deer would quake with fear and run away from the king and his cook.

The king of the Banyan deer called for a meeting with the king of the Monkey deer. "My friend, many of the deer from both of our herds are full of terror. They are being killed for all to see. Not only that, many of our deer are left wounded when the arrows don't hit their mark. What can we do about this situation?"

The two kings brought their advisers and discussed possible ways to prevent this sad situation. One of the deer kings suggested, "Why don't we have one deer from my herd go up to be killed one day and the next day, one from your herd will go up. That way there won't be any wounded and fewer deer will be killed."

"That is a good plan," the king of the Monkey deer herd said. And so, each day, a deer from the herd of the day would go and lie down and place its head on a block of carved wood that they brought to the park. The cook would come and chop the head off, then take the body to use in cooking.

Then, one sad day, a mother deer that had a young baby was the one selected to place her head on the block. Before that could happen, she went to her king and begged, "Oh king of the Monkey deer. Today is my turn to place my head on the block and be killed for the cook to use in dishes for the king. I beg you to let my turn pass until my baby is old enough to survive on his own without me." The king of the Monkey deer looked at her and she continued, "When my baby is old enough, I will then go and place my head on the block."

The Monkey deer king listened, but he decided not to help her. "Your lot has turned up that you are to die today. There is no other way out of it."

The desperate mother deer went to the king of the Banyan deer and begged the same thing of him. "Please dear king, do not have me be the deer killed today. I have a young baby who is not able to survive yet on his own. Spare me today and when my baby is grown up enough to make it by himself, I will willingly put my head on the block."

The Banyan deer, with eyes the color of gold, shed a tear. "Go back to your herd, little mother. I myself will go in your place instead."

And so it was that the next day the cook found the king of the Banyan deer with his head on the block, and couldn't kill it. He returned to the king of the people. "Oh king, you must help me with a problem. I went to the park today to kill the deer of the day, but found the king of the Banyan deer herd with his head on the chopping block. I could not kill him. What am I to do?"

"I'll take care of this myself," the king declared. He went to the park and sure enough, there was the king of the Banyan deer herd with his neck on the block. "Banyan deer king. Never have I seen such compassion and love as you have shown for the mother deer. Your kindness and mercy are truly royal and rare. I order you to rise up. I will grant you your life this day and the mother deer's as well. From this day forth, I will never hunt the deer again either in this park or in the forest. Go, run free."

Old Badger and Old Frog
(Native American, California, USA)

Back in the ancient times when frogs had teeth, Old Badger was very thirsty, but he had problems getting around. He just could not get to water to get enough to drink. His friend, Old Frog, promised to get him all he wanted to drink.

Old Frog began to gnaw upon a big tree. He kept on gnawing until he had drawn out all the sap, which he carefully put into a hollow place. Then he helped Old Badger get to this hollow place, but it just couldn't hold enough water to quench his thirst.

Old Frog went to the young frogs. "Young frogs, we need your help. Old Badger can't get around to where the water is and he is thirsty. Help me dig out a place and make a big hollow in the ground."

The young frogs quickly agreed, and they began to dig out a place. They dug, and dug, and dug, until they had made a great big hollow in the ground. All the creatures joined in the effort to fill that hollow with water for Old Badger. When they finally got it filled, Old Badger had enough to drink.

That place is filled with water to this day and is named Clear Lake.

Thoughts About the Stories, Discussions, and Activities

THE BADGER'S MONEY

This is the story of an old priest who has given up the riches of the world for contemplation. He gives aid to a badger and together they give each other compassion and gratitude as they share their lives.

- ⊙ *In this story, the priest takes compassion upon a badger. Eventually the badger insists upon repaying the favors. Do you think most compassionate actions are repaid? If so, discuss how. If not, discuss why.*
- ⊙ *Do you think it is easier to have compassionate feelings toward animals than it is toward other humans? Why or why not?*

ARION AND HIS HARP

In this tale, a display of greed and lack of compassion backfires on a group of men. Amazingly, compassion is exhibited by creatures of the sea.

- ⊙ *Research stories of dolphins in the library or on the Internet. There are many true stories of how dolphins have helped people throughout the world. Write an essay about their friendship with humans.*

⊙ *After doing the research in the above activity, discuss whether or not you think this story might be based in truth.*

THE GRATEFUL FOXES

This is another tale of animal characters that present compassion and caring for others.

⊙ *In this story, compassion is repaid with compassion. Can you think of any instances in your life when you were in this type of situation? Write a story about it.*

⊙ *How can people repay those, unrelated to them, who come forward and provide them with the help they need? Brainstorm possible ideas.*

THE FOX AND THE HORSE

This story shows how loyal, hardworking traits can be repaid by those without compassion for what is around them.

⊙ *Reread the story. Can you identify any parallel instances as displayed in this story with real life examples?*

⊙ *How are the old and infirm cared for in your community? Is respect and compassion shown to them? How is this evident? Brainstorm a list of ideas on what more could be done.*

THE GOLDEN LION

Three sons take different approaches to a challenge. The youngest son does not enter the search for the young princess for his own profit, but to relieve his father's mind. He shows compassion to an old beggar woman and is rewarded.

⊙ *Each of the three sons in this story makes the same journey, but with different motives. What are the motives of each? Do you think motives can determine success or failure? Can you offer any examples of this from your own life?*

⊙ *Why was the youngest son able to succeed on his mission? What actions helped him? Create a storyboard or comic-strip style illustration of this story to map the actions of the characters.*

THE DEER OF INDIA

In this story, kind and merciful deer are pitted against the power of a king. Life and death is the issue. Without force, the deer show the king what true compassion really is.

- *A deer king demonstrates compassion and leadership in this tale by offering to sacrifice his own life. Wild animals sometimes sacrifice their lives for their young. Research animal behavior in the library or on the Internet to find instances of this, and write a report about it.*
- *Is compassion a trait that leaders should have? Which world leaders have shown compassion? Make a list, then choose one and write a brief biography of that person, emphasizing their compassion.*

OLD BADGER AND OLD FROG

In this story, compassion is shown to the old and infirm.

- *Water is used as a symbol in this story. What other symbols are there for compassion and kindness? Choose one and write a poem using it.*
- *Compassion becomes a group effort in this story. Brainstorm a list of ways that you could express compassion with a group.*

Other Activity Ideas

- *The events of September 11, 2001 impacted the whole world. As a result, people have shown compassion for those they know as well as for total strangers.*

  - *Identify and list expressions of compassion from the news about this disaster.*
  - *How did the mayor of New York and the president of the United States demonstrate compassion for the devastation?*
  - *After the bombing, musicians came forth with outpourings of comfort and hope. Did their efforts show their compassion? How are music and art related to compassion? Cite some examples that demonstrate your points.*
  - *Has the compassion following 9/11 lasted?*

- *Make a compassion scrapbook. Include in it:*

  - *clippings from your local newspaper that demonstrate compassion*
  - *stories about compassion based on interviews with students, parents, friends*
  - *your own stories about compassion—when it was shown to you and when you felt compassion for others*
  - *stories about compassion found on the Internet*

- *How do stories in books present compassion? Make a list of books, stories, poems, and their contribution to developing compassion in the reader/listener.*
- *How do groups and organizations show compassion toward animals in our society? On the Internet or in the library, research organizations that help animals, and write a report about one of them.*
- *Discuss possible ways to work with hospitals, nursing homes, and retirement homes to study and implement actions involving compassion.*
- *Parents often exhibit compassion in their own homes with night-lights and stuffed animals to comfort young children. Look around you and list any other everyday ways you see evidence of this feeling.*
- *Imagine and draw or make a stuffed animal that you think would encourage compassion.*
- *Stories and books shared with children before bedtime become remembered moments. Can you recall any stories or books that shared the thoughts of compassion along with this nighttime ritual?*
- *List some of the common symbols used in our society that contribute to and promote compassion.*
- *What are some blessings from cultures throughout the world that encourage compassion? Create a book of blessings and illustrate each of them. For example, investigate the custom of sharing blessings with the string-tying ceremony of the Hmong. On important events such as marriage, graduation, or birthdays, friends and family each tie a string around the wrist of the person being honored and give a blessing to them as they do it. (For further information on this, explore string tying in* Folk Stories of the Hmong: Peoples of Laos, Thailand and Vietnam *by Norma J. Livo and Dia Cha, Libraries Unlimited, 1991; and* Teaching with Folk Stories of the Hmong *by Dia Cha and Norma J. Livo, Libraries Unlimited, 2000.)*
- *Stories help make us more human by allowing us to live more lives than we have. They help us see the world from inside the skins of people different from ourselves. Give examples of some stories that have taught you compassion and given insight into the behavior of yourself and others.*
- *Create a reader's theatre or puppet script from a story you know that includes a narrator, characters, and action that express compassion. Present it for others. Collect all such reader's theatre scripts into a book.*

⊙ *The story of "Cinderella" can be found in the literature of many cultures. See how many versions you can find in your library. Why do you think these stories are so popular and have traveled and survived for so long? How does this story illustrate compassion?*

See the "General Activities" section at the end of this book for ideas to further explore these topics.

Responsibility

The Little Red Hen
(United States)

Little Red Hen lived in the barnyard with her three little chicks and her friends—the cat, the dog, the pig, and the duck. One morning, while she was pecking around on the ground, she found some grains of wheat. She went to her friends and asked, "Who will help me plant the seeds?"

"Not I," said the cat.

"Not I," said the dog.

"Not I," said the pig.

"Not I," said the duck.

"Then I will do it myself," said Little Red Hen. And she did. The grains of wheat sprouted and grew into tall ripe stalks of wheat. She went to her friends and asked, "Who will help me cut these stalks of wheat?"

"Not I," said the cat.

"Not I," said the dog.

"Not I," said the pig.

"Not I," said the duck.

"Then I will do it myself," said Little Red Hen. And she did. Next, Little Red Hen went to her friends and asked, "Who will help me thresh this wheat?"

"Not I," said the cat.

"Not I," said the dog.

"Not I," said the pig.

"Not I," said the duck.

"Then I will do it myself," said Little Red Hen. And she did. Next, Little Red Hen went to her friends and asked, "Who will help me grind these grains of wheat into flour?"

"Not I," said the cat.

"Not I," said the dog.

"Not I," said the pig.

"Not I," said the duck.

"Then I will do it myself," said Little Red Hen. And she did. Next, Little Red Hen went to her friends and asked, "Who will help me bake this flour into bread?"

"Not I," said the cat.

"Not I," said the dog.

"Not I," said the pig.

"Not I," said the duck.

"Then I will do it myself," said Little Red Hen. And she did. After the bread was baked and out of the oven, Little Red Hen called to her friends and asked, "Who will help me eat this bread?"

"I will," said the cat.

"I will," said the dog.

"I will," said the pig.

"I will," said the duck.

"Oh no," said Little Red Hen. "My chicks and I will eat the bread." And they did.

The Three Shirts of Bog Cotton
(Scotland)

There once was a king who had three handsome sons and a beautiful daughter. His wife had died and after a few years he grew so lonely, he decided to marry again. The children were still young and they got along well enough with the king's new wife.

Then, one day, an ancient, frightful, bad woman named Each-lair Urlair arrived from her travels throughout the country. She sought out the new queen and asked, "How are you and the king getting along?"

"Very well," answered the queen with a smile.

"Och, yes. And how are you and the children … ?"

"We get along fine," said the queen. "I treat them, the sweet things, exactly as if they were my very own children."

The evil woman looked at the queen through squinting eyes, "Indeed!" she said. "You are very foolish!"

"And just why is that?" demanded the queen.

"Ha!" said the evil woman, who was starting to look uglier as every moment passed. "Supposing the king died tomorrow. Your share of this place wouldn't come to very much."

"The good lord knows," said the queen, "that I would never do any harm to the children regardless of what may become of me here."

"Oh now, you needn't do anything wrong," hissed the evil woman. "You send them up to me and you shall not be to blame for anything."

"I don't know about that," answered the queen. "The four of them are delightful children."

The evil one just kept insisting and telling the queen that, "You are being silly. Send them up to me tomorrow. When you do, ask them to come to my home for the yellow comb. Tell them they are going on an errand to get the yellow comb," wheedled the old woman.

And that is just how it happened the very next day. The king was off hunting in the mountains, so the queen sent the oldest boy off, telling him, "Go up to the house of Eachlair Urlair and ask her to give you the yellow comb. Bring it back down to me." The lad left, not suspecting anything. He traveled up to the house of Eachlair Urlair and knocked at her door.

"Come in," instructed the evil woman's voice. He went in and she asked him, "What do you want my dear?"

"My stepmother the queen sent me here," he answered. "She wants me to get the yellow comb."

"Oh yes," the old woman replied. "There it is over there on that dresser. Take it."

When the lad went across the room to the dresser, he could see the comb was there. As he picked it up, Eachlair Urlair struck him with her magic wand and he was transformed into a black raven. He turned to leave. As he was crossing the threshold, he spat out a mouthful of blood and flew off away from the house.

Time passed and the queen could see there was no sign of the son coming home, so she said to the second-oldest boy, "Goodness. Your brother has not come back yet. You had better go up to see where he is and tell him to come home. If you do not see him, go to the house of Eachlair Urlair and ask her for the yellow comb."

This son set off for the house of the wicked woman. When his brother, the raven, saw him coming, he began to continuously dart at him, until it seemed like he would take his head off. The lad started to run and tried to get into the house of Eachlair Urlair before the raven could harm him. He opened the door and breathlessly went in. "Has my brother been here?"

"Oh no, my dear," replied the squinty-eyed woman.

"Well then, the queen asked him to come up here to get the yellow comb," he said.

"No one has been here at all," said the old woman. "There is the comb over on the dresser. Just go and take it." When the poor unsuspecting boy was almost at the dresser, Eachlair Urlair swung around with the magic wand and he was changed into another black raven. Out he flew from the house, as his brother had done. When he left, he saw the blood at the door and he too spat out a mouthful of blood beside it.

The two brothers joined up, both uneasy about getting back home. At this very moment, the third brother was being sent to Eachlair Urlair's house by the queen. As he came along the trail, the two ravens flapped their wings and dove at him. They were not quite striking him, but darting so closely, they got in his way from head to toe. All this third brother could do was run and try to get inside before these ravens could harm him. He rushed into the house and asked Eachlair Urlair, "Were my brothers here? The queen sent both of them up to get the yellow comb," he told her.

"Well, no indeed my dear," she said. "None of your brothers have been here. Are you sure they were to come up here?"

"Yes," said the third brother. "I myself heard my stepmother send them up here."

"Oh, neither of them have been here," she told the boy. "The comb is over there on the dresser. Go across and take it." The poor boy did as she said. Just as it had happened to his two brothers, he was struck by the wand and changed into another black raven.

Their sister, who was the oldest of the children, became anxious about her brothers. "My three brothers left quite a time ago and they are still not back from the errand. I am worried."

The queen looked at her innocently and said, "Goodness. You had better go see what has happened to the lads." So, the sister left in search of her brothers. When the three ravens saw her coming along the trail, they flew in a frenzy around her. Before she got to the house, it occurred to her that something was not right. Arriving at the door, she noticed the three mouthfuls of blood on the threshold. She went in and asked Eachlair Urlair, "Have you seen any sign of my three brothers here today?"

"Oh no, my dear," said the evil one. "Were they supposed to come here?"

"Are you sure you haven't seen them?" persisted the sister.

"Oh no," answered the woman.

"But our stepmother asked them to come up here to get the yellow comb," explained the sister.

"They have not been here at all," insisted the evil one. "They probably just got interested in something along the way and at any rate, they never got here," persisted Eachlair Urlair. "The yellow comb is over there on the dresser. Go across, my dearie, and take it."

The girl started toward the dresser, but she was keeping an eye on the woman, who was behind her. When she saw her lifting the magic wand, the sister sprang at the woman and seized the wand from her. She struck Eachlair Urlair with it on the crown of her head. "You can just stay there," the sister told the evil one, and turned her into a pillar of stone.

She turned and left the house without even taking the comb. Crossing the threshold, she again noticed the three mouthfuls of blood. Carefully, she took them up and wrapped them in her handkerchief. Outside, the three ravens flew about her in joy that she had made it out of the house. By this time, it was almost nightfall.

The ravens headed south and their sister followed them. When it got dark, she was able to trail them by listening carefully to where they were croaking in the sky above her. Then, she lost them, and as she was looking around her, she saw a light and headed straight for it. She came to a house and knocked at the door, but there was no response. She carefully opened the door, went in, and sat down at a table that was there. She decided to wait and see if anyone was at home or living in the house, but no one appeared. The girl just sat there until she heard the croaking of the ravens coming toward the house. They flew in, and then each one of them cast off his raven coverings. The three brothers joined her at the table.

"Thank goodness, sister, that you got away safely," the oldest brother said.

"Oh yes," she answered.

There was food on the table, so they all had a meal, then gathered around. "Is there anything in the world," she asked them, "that can break the spell that binds you?"

The oldest brother said, "Oh, yes. There is one thing, but I don't suppose you will be able to do it."

"Let me decide," she told him. "Let me hear what it is."

"It is this," he quietly said. "I have seen it in writing. You must make a shirt of bog cotton for each one of us, and from the day that you begin to pick the bog cotton to the day when you say, 'Health to wear your shirt, sweet brother,' you must not utter one single, solitary word in that time."

"Well then," she said, "we shall see what can be done."

When daylight came, the ravens left, and their sister got the house in order. Nobody came to disturb her. She took off for the hills and picked a sack full of bog cotton that day. When she was done, she just left the cotton where she had picked it and came back to the house.

Her brothers returned, threw off their coverings, and turned into young fellows. They came into the room and began to try and catch her, to see if they could get her to speak. Not a syllable could they get out of her all night long.

The next morning, they left; she got the house cleaned up, and went to the hills. The sister picked another sack full of bog cotton that day, put it alongside the one from the day before, and then left to go back to the house. Her brothers returned and again tried to make her speak, but not a syllable could they get out of her.

The next morning, as soon as they had eaten their meal, the brothers left again. The girl went earlier this day to see if she could pick a sack full of bog cotton and carry it near to the road. She was busy picking all the day, then decided that since it was fairly early in the evening, she would start to carry the sacks to the road. She managed to get the three sacks there, but by this time it was so dark that she could not make out which way she ought to go to get back to the house. "My brothers will only be tormenting me anyway if I were to go home," she thought, and decided to wait right there in the shelter of the sacks until it was daylight.

Suddenly, she heard hoofbeats. A horseman, sensing something as he passed, stopped and spoke to her. She did not make a sound. He asked at least two or three times who she was. "Why are you here at this time? Are you in trouble?" When she did not reply, he finally lifted her up, set her behind him on his horse, and off they went. They traveled on for some time until arriving at his house. He helped her down, put the horse in the stable, and brought her into the house.

"Look mother," he called out, "I found this woman along the road and she cannot speak a word. There were some sacks of bog cotton beside her along the road. I will have to bring them home."

The horseman was a gentleman, a great man. His house was quite a fine one, and he and his mother were concerned for the girl. When they went to bed, she got a room all to herself. The next morning, he left to get the sacks and brought them home. No sooner had he done this than she set to work with the bog cotton. She carded it and worked it and spun it on a distaff.

She and the gentleman fell in love and were married. She became pregnant, but still kept working away at the shirts. The night before she gave birth to her baby, she had the first shirt finished. She folded it carefully and put it in a chest in her room. That night, she gave birth to a baby boy, Before morning came, however, there was no trace of the child. He had been stolen. Someone suggested to her husband that she had killed the child and that there was no figuring what she had done with it. Her husband said that for the time at least, nothing would be done to her. "She is not only beautiful, but a good person," he told everyone.

After the girl started to feel better, she began working on the second shirt. She carded and combed the cotton, spun it, and did all the work that had to be done. She became pregnant a second time, and the night before she delivered, she folded the second shirt and put it away alongside the first one.

In spite of the fact that there were midwives and women about the place, before daybreak the baby boy also was stolen. It was again suggested to her husband that she must be responsible for this missing child. He told them, "Well, we shall let her be this time again." People gossiped about her, saying that since she didn't speak at all it was clear that she was not normal. Yet, on the other hand, she was such a good worker, maybe she was normal after all.

When she had recovered for the second time, she began working on the third shirt. Amazingly, she became pregnant once more and again, the night before she gave birth, she folded the third shirt and put it away in the chest with the others. The next night, she gave birth to another boy, but the following morning, there was so sign of the newborn baby. It too had disappeared.

Everyone kept after her husband, telling him his wife was evil, and finally he decided that she should be burned. A crowd gathered, and just when it was time for her to be brought out, three horsemen who were her brothers drew near. The first horseman came up and had a child about three years old in his arms. The second horseman had a child about two years old in his arms and the third horseman had a baby in front of him on the horse.

The one who was holding the oldest child dismounted and asked, "What is the meaning of all of this?" The husband explained everything that had happened. "May I have a word with this woman myself and my brothers here?" asked the horseman.

"Indeed you may," said the gentleman. "You may have a word with her and take her away with you if you wish to. Indeed, I hate to have to go and do something as violent as having her burned. Yes, come in here."

The girl was sent up, and she and her three brothers and the three children gathered in the room. Her husband left and closed the door behind him. They locked the door on the inside. The sister went across the room to her chest, took out the first shirt she had made, and gave it to her oldest brother. He put the shirt on and she said to him, "Health to wear your shirt, sweet brother."

"Good health to you, sweet sister," he said. "Here is your first child."

When her husband outside the door heard her speaking, he demanded they open the door. "It is not to be opened yet," said the oldest brother.

She brought out the second shirt and gave it to her brother. He undressed and put it on. "Health to wear your shirt, sweet brother," she said.

"Good health to you, sweet sister," he said, "and here is your second son."

Again, her husband demanded to be let in, but they would not open the door. He burst through the door and declared, "Although I had everyone here who has ever lived, you are certainly not going away. Now that I know that you can speak, you will stay where you are," he said.

The girl motioned for him to stand back for a moment until her third brother received his shirt. She got the shirt and gave it to her brother. He undressed and put it on. "Health to wear your shirt, sweet brother," she said.

"Good health to you, sweet sister," he answered her. "Here is your baby who was born last night."

She took the baby and cuddled it. The brothers and their sister told the gentleman the whole story of Eachlair Urlair from beginning to end. All that remained to be done was to clear away the crowd outside that had been there waiting to see the woman being burned.

The maiden and her husband were married again with their three sons and her brothers as witnesses. Then, the three brothers went with their sister and her family to the house of their father, the king.

The king had become sick after the disappearance of his children, but when he was rejoined with them, he miraculously recovered. They told their father of their adventures. The king sent the stepmother to the house of Eachlair Urlair. "Strike her with the wand and wake her up," he told her. "Change her back from the pillar of stone to what she had been before and bring her back to me."

When this was done, the king declared, "The queen and Eachlair Urlair are to be burned and their ashes scattered to the winds." It was done.

The sister and her family went back to their house, where her brothers stayed on with them. It was a happy home with the married couple, their three sons, her three brothers, and the man's mother. And not only did the joyful girl speak, but she sang songs of happiness daily.

The Sage Grouse
(Paiute, North America)

Once upon a long, long time ago, when mice ran after cats and rats chased lions, most of the world was underwater except for the very top of a mountain. Way up on the mountain's summit were the last remains of fire in the entire universe. This fire burned brightly there, and flickered on the clouds in the sky.

The Paiutes, who had lived through the great storms and floods, knew that their only hope of survival was to get to the fire, which was high above them. But reaching it wouldn't be easy because storms raged and roared from the sky itself, and waves of water came close to putting the fire out.

Finally, when all the people had become depressed and had given up all hope, a little prairie chicken flew to the tip of the mountain and sat close to the fire, fanning the embers to keep it alive. This brave little bird constantly protected the precious fire from the drenching waves of the flood as they swept and splashed nearby.

The little bird fought the waves, fanned the fire, and was constantly on alert to danger. She managed to save the fire, but she paid dearly for her efforts. She had sat, danced, and fanned her wings so close to the fire that it scorched her breast—and to this day the little bird carries a black breast to remind everyone of her bravery and determination.

The words I have spoken, which you have now heard, you will hear tomorrow when a bird speaks them.

Note: Reprinted from *Celebrating the Earth: Stories, Experiences, and Activities* by Norma J. Livo ©2000 Libraries Unlimited.

Thoughts About the Stories, Discussions, and Activities

THE LITTLE RED HEN

This well-known tale shows us the difference between those who work and those who assume they will reap the results of the work. The simple lesson is that if we expect to share, we should accept the responsibility of helping too.

- ⊙ *What are some of the tasks you perform at school and at home in order to share in the benefits they provide? Make a list and share.*
- ⊙ *Have you ever felt like the only one working on a project that will benefit many? Write a story about it using the format of "The Little Red Hen."*

THE THREE SHIRTS OF BOG COTTON

A sister assumes the responsibility of transforming her brothers back into their human form. In doing this, she faces problems and danger, but she perseveres.

- ⊙ *The sister in this story demonstrates not only great responsibility, but also tremendous self-discipline. Discuss how these two traits are related, using examples from the story or from your own experience.*
- ⊙ *This story involves a betrayal by the stepmother. What lesson does it teach us about the responsibilities of stepparents?*

THE SAGE GROUSE

A little bird brings fire from the top of the mountain when others cannot accomplish this task. She assumes the responsibility.

- ⊙ *What does the phrase "keep the home fires burning" mean, and how is it related to responsibility? Why was keeping the fire so important to the Paiutes?*
- ⊙ *Research in the library or on the Internet to learn more about the sage grouse or prairie chicken. Illustrate a scene from the story that includes the bird.*

Other Activity Ideas

⊙ Do you accept responsibility and challenges? Discuss ways that teachers motivate you to do better in your work.

⊙ A common saying is that for every action there is a reaction. Brainstorm with others how our actions contribute to personal responsibility.

⊙ List three responsibilities you are ready to assume. Then choose one and write five reasons why you should be given that responsibility. Present your list of reasons to your parent or teacher.

⊙ Institute "class meetings" or group meetings in which participants discuss topics such as conflicts or achievements, either personal or with a group.

   ⊙ What is a responsible way to react to conflict?
   ⊙ How can each person contribute to group achievement in a positive, responsible way?

⊙ Review the stories in this section and list the ways the characters exhibited responsibility.

⊙ Write an original story about a time you took responsibility. (If this is done as a group project, bind the collected stories into a book to be shared with others.) Find other stories and characters that exhibit the trait of responsibility in your school or public library. Develop a bibliography of these to be included in the group book.

⊙ *What can students take responsibility for that will improve the school? Make a list of possible choices, then take a class vote and decide how to accomplish the goal.*

See the "General Activities" section at the back of this book for more ideas to further explore these topics.

Cooperation

The Lion and the Mouse
(Aesop)

A huge lion was chased through the jungle by hunters, but managed to escape. He lay sleeping under a shady tree, tired out from the chase. Some mice saw him sleeping there and bravely scrambled over him. When their movement on his fur woke him up, he snatched out a paw, caught one of them, and was about to crush him.

"Please spare my life, oh lion," pleaded the squeaking mouse. "I meant you no harm." The lion took pity on the mouse and let him go.

The moon rose and set several times, and the lion now found himself caught in a net laid by some hunters. No matter how hard he strained and struggled in the net, he was unable to free himself. The only thing he could do was fill the forest with the sound of his anguished, angry roars.

Nearby, the mouse whose life the lion had spared heard the roars. He came and gnawed through the ropes with his sharp little teeth. The lion and the mouse looked at each other in gratitude.

Lessons from a Father
(Tennessee, USA)

A hardworking farmer in east Tennessee was feeling all the aches and pains of hard work, along with his advanced age. As he lay sick in bed, he knew that he was about to die. He gathered his four sons and three daughters around his bed.

All seven of his children had inherited his flaming red hair. "We are a family with much alike in us all and yet with many strong differences," he spoke. "It is time for me to give you a dying father's advice. You all will inherit our land equally. There is enough land with good soil to grow things for all," he said softly. "I will now share with you one of the most important things of all for you to remember in the future."

He turned to the youngest of his children, "Go outside and gather a fistful of dry sticks from the rowan tree in front and bring them here to me." The child followed the instructions quickly and handed the sticks to his father. The farmer, with a twinkle still left in his eyes, handed them to the middle child. "Clutch them in the middle tightly and break them," he said. The middle child tried with all of his might, grunted and growled, but could not break them.

Next, the father told the middle child, "Now fling them on the floor." The son, with a quizzical look on his face, did as his father had told him. He flung all the sticks on the floor.

"Take each of these sticks," the father said quietly. "Break them one by one." Of course, the son was able to do this with ease.

"This is the most important lesson I can give you," smiled the father. "If you are united, you will all prosper, but if you are not, if you each go in his or her own way, you will fail as a family."

The Hunt
(Aesop)

A lion had been watching three oxen feeding in an open field. He tried to attack them several times, but they stayed together, helped protect each other, and successfully drove him off. The lion was no match for these three strong oxen with their sharp horns and fierce hooves, but he was hungry and found it hard to resist the chance to snag one of them for his meal.

As the day wore on, the lion could see that there was little chance of getting that meal. Then, as he was lurking and waiting, one of the oxen quarreled with another. The hungry lion crept in close to watch them, licking his chops the whole time.

Finally, luck was on the lion's side. He found the oxen in separate corners of the field. They were as far away from one another as they could get.

It was now an easy matter for the lion to attack the oxen one at a time. He proceeded to do this with the greatest satisfaction and relish.

The Escape of the Pigeons
(Persia)

A fowler was laying his snares to catch pigeons in the middle of a wood. A raven watched him with beady eyes from a bough as he placed the snares under a tree and sprinkled a handful of grain beneath the net for bait. After he had done this, the fowler walked away.

A flock of pigeons wheeled in the sky above the wood. The raven croaked, "Brothers, beware, beware! The grain you see there was put by the bird-catcher to trap you. Beware!"

But the greedy pigeons did not pay any attention to the raven. "You only say that because you envy us our grain," they cried. And so, they swarmed down on the grain and were instantly caught in the fowler's net.

In despair the pigeons cried, "Woe to us! Woe to us! The raven's words were true. Why, oh why, did we not believe him! Woe to us," they cried. In vain they beat their wings against the net until they were weary, but they could not get free.

The pigeons could see the fowler in the distance, hurrying toward them! Now in mortal fear, they remembered the raven and wailed to him, "Raven, raven. Please forgive us and help us!"

"I ought to just leave you to your fate," replied the raven. "However, I feel sorry for you. Listen carefully to me then. Stop beating your wings uselessly, and use your wings to all fly up together. The net will rise with you. I will lead you to my friend the mouse who will gnaw the net through."

The desperate pigeons obeyed. They gathered up all their strength, gave a signal, and soared up into the sky taking the net with them just as the raven had said.

The fowler could only stand there helplessly, under the trees, and watch as the net and pigeons disappeared from sight.

The Great Canoe
(Maori, New Zealand)

This is the story of what happened when Rata cut down a tree without telling the god of the forest. Rata planned to make a great canoe, which is a good thing to love. When a canoe is well made, it becomes alive. It is a gift from the forest god, and it becomes a living thing of the sea god.

Rata searched and searched the forest until he found the exact tree to make his great canoe. It was so straight and tall that it cast a shadow on all of the forest around it. It was broad and proud. Rata knew that this was the only tree that was good enough for the canoe he saw in his mind.

He drew out his adze with its sharp edge and started to cut the great tree. Thump! Thump! Whack! Thud! He sweated all afternoon with his efforts to cut the tree down. Finally, the tree fell with an earth-shaking thud. Rata then proceeded to cut off all of the branches and leaves. "What a grand canoe this tree will be!" he said, as he finished his work for the day.

Rata went home, ate, and went to bed. While he slept the deep sleep of someone who had worked hard that day, strange things were happening. The spirits of the forest had become angry that the incredible tree had been cut down. The spirits called all of the birds, insects, and little people of the bush together. In a great effort, they all tugged at the great tree. As they worked, the tree moved on its grassy bed. The sounds of whirring wings filled the air. Slowly, slowly, slowly, the tree was pulled upright again and once more stood in its own place in the forest.

The tiny insects carried the chips and grains of wood from the ground and fitted them in place. As they worked, they sang:

Fly together, ships and shavings,
Stick fast together,
Hold fast together,
Stand upright again, O tree!

Rata eagerly returned in the morning to start shaping the canoe. He couldn't believe his eyes, for as he looked around he saw broken twigs and leaves and the rut where the tree had fallen into the ground. He thought that maybe he had made a mistake, but there was no mistake about it. The tree stood once again where it had been growing for ages.

Rata knew the spirits had done it, so he sang a song of magic to protect himself. Again, he took up his adze and labored for the long, hot afternoon to cut the tree down. Once more, it fell, and he again took off the branches and leaves. He removed shavings from the trunk and smoothed its surface. It was now nightfall and the shape of the canoe was visible. He needed to hollow out the hull to finish it. He gathered up his adze and went home again for the night.

The next morning, there was no sign of his previous day's work. Once again, the birds and insects had raised the tree during the night. There it stood, tall and proud, towering over the other trees of the forest.

Rata chopped the tree down for a third time. Then, instead of working on shaping the canoe again, he took his adze and walked back toward the village. When he was out of sight of the tree, he turned around and slipped quietly through the deep ferns until he could see the tree on the ground. As darkness drew nigh, he heard the birds and insects singing:

Fly together, chips and shavings,
Stick fast together,
Hold fast together,
Stand upright again, O tree!

He watched and saw the flash of the wings of more forest birds than he had ever seen before. All of the birds—Weka, Kiwi, Fantail, Ruru, Kaka, and Kakapo—were pulling, and tugging, and working to get the great tree back to its standing position. Rata watched all the insects working steadily to help. He felt the strength of the magic song, as his own feet seemed to leave the ground.

The tree rose upward, almost obscured by the fluttering wings of the thousands of birds. Once again, it stood straight with its cut surface standing on the stump. Insects swarmed to fit the tiny splinters, shavings, chips, and grains of wood back into place again.

Rata sprang up and rushed toward the tree, "Ha! Now I see who has spoiled all of my work."

"So, it was you, Rata, who dared to kill the heart of this tree!" the birds called to him.

"What shall I do?" asked Rata, now feeling ashamed. "I wanted a canoe that I could use to travel far over the sea on a sacred journey. My father died in a distant land and I want to bring his body back to his homeland. That is the reason I cut down this tree."

"Go back to your home, Rata," all the birds and insects cried and buzzed. "We will make you a canoe that will take you on your journey."

Rata left the forest and returned home; he knew the tiny forest people would keep their word. The next morning, he returned to the spot in the forest he knew so well and there was a canoe, "Riwara," or the Great Joy.

That wasn't all that the forest people did. They dragged the canoe through the forest on sapling skids and launched it on the sea. There, it rode proud and stately, big enough to hold 140 men. It was then that the fighting men of Rata took their places in the canoe and put their shoulders to the paddles. The Riwara skimmed the waves like a gull flying above the water and lifting the canoe to the incoming waves.

Stealing Fire
(Native American, Oregon, USA)

Many, many moons ago, people did not know how to make fire. At that time, there was only one fire in all the world—on top of a great mountain. There were three guardians of the fire, who would not let anyone take it away or even come near it to get warm. The winter was very cold, and all the people and creatures suffered greatly.

Then, Coyote summoned all the animals to a council and sent Wren to call the birds. He told them that he felt sorry for the people who had neither feathers nor fur to keep them warm. He thought the animals ought to try to get fire for themselves. Very few of the animals had ever seen fire, and they asked many foolish questions. Coyote, Raven, and Old Crow tried to explain, but they could not make the animals understand. Grizzly said, "If you bring fire down here, I'll eat him."

Coyote realized that if there were to be any fire, he would have to get it himself. He went up to the mountaintop and waited for a long, long, time. Finally, the guardian who was watching the fire went away, and the one who was to take his place was not quite ready.

Taking advantage of this opportunity, Coyote grabbed some fire and ran. He did not get very far before a guardian saw him and called out an alarm. All three guardians began to chase him down the mountainside. One of them came so near that he caught hold of the tip of Coyote's tail and held it so hard that it turned white. That is why, to this day, Coyote has a white tip on his tail.

Coyote saw that he could not get away, so he threw the fire to Wolf. Wolf took it and ran down the mountainside. When one of the guardians caught up with him, Wolf saw that he could not get away and threw the fire to Squirrel. Squirrel took it and ran up in the treetops. The guardian was not able to follow him, but the fire was so hot that it scorched Squirrel and curled up his tail. To this day, Squirrel has a black spot on his neck and his tail curls up.

Squirrel was able to throw the fire to Frog, who took it and hopped away. A guardian caught up with Frog and grabbed his tail. When Frog hopped away, his tail came off in the guardian's hand. That is why Frog has no tail to this day.

The guardian again caught up to Frog, who threw the fire to Wood. Wood swallowed it. The guardian did not know how to get the fire out of Wood, so he went away.

Coyote took two pieces of the wood that held the fire and rubbed them against each other. He rubbed a long, long time. At last the wood began to get warm. It got warmer and warmer, until finally a spark came out.

After that, people never needed to suffer again with the cold. They knew they could always get fire out of wood by rubbing two pieces against each other.

The Crane and the Wood Grouse
(Finland)

There once was a crane that carried all the little birds, snug on his back, to the warm land over the waters. Once it happened that the wood grouse joined the crane on his way to the shore, and the grouse said, "Carry me on your back!"

The crane said, "I am not strong enough to carry you across the waters." And they went together until they arrived at the shore.

Once they reached the sea, the wood grouse got off the crane, perched, and stared in awe, for she couldn't see land on the other side. "I will not go to that distant land over the waters," she said. "I would rather stay here and lie in the snow and eat shoots of the plants. They don't cut down the spruce trees here, and there are many pine trees on the hill." With that, she turned away and walked back from the shore. The crane and its remaining passengers took off and slowly were lost from sight as they traveled out over the immense waters.

That is why the wood grouse lies in the snow and eats pine shoots to this very day.

Long, Broad, and Sharpsight
(Slavonic)

Once upon a time, there was a king, who was already old, and had but one son. He called this son to him and said, "My dear son! You know that old fruit falls to make room for other fruit. My head is already ripening, and maybe the sun will soon no longer shine upon it. Before you bury me, I should like to see your wife, my future daughter. My son, marry!"

The prince replied, "I would gladly, father, do as you wish, but I have no bride and don't know any."

The old king put his hand into his pocket and took out a golden key. He showed it to his son, with the words, "Go up into the tower, to the top story, look round there and then tell me which you fancy."

The prince went without delay. No one within the memory of man had ever been up in the tower or heard what was there. When he got up to the last story, he saw in the ceiling a little iron door like a trapdoor. It was closed, but he opened it with the golden key, lifted it, and went up.

There was a large, circular room. The ceiling was blue like the sky on a clear night, and silver stars glittered on it. The floor held a carpet of green silk, and around the wall were twelve high windows in golden frames. In each window on crystal glass was a damsel painted with the colors of the rainbow. Each one was wearing a different dress and royal crown on her head, and each was lovelier than the next. It was a wonder that the prince did not let his eyes dwell on them. While he gazed at them with astonishment, the damsels began to move as if they were alive, looked down upon him, smiled, and did everything but speak.

The prince observed that one of the twelve windows was covered with a white curtain. He drew the curtain to see what was behind it. There was a damsel in a white dress with a silver dirndl and a crown of pearls on her head. She was the most beautiful of all, but was sad and pale. It was almost as if she had risen from the grave. The prince stood long before the picture, as if he had made a discovery. As he gazed, his heart pained him, and he cried, "This one will I have as a wife and no other." As he said the words, the damsel bowed her head, blushed like a rose, and—at that instant—all the pictures disappeared.

When he went down and related to his father what he had seen and which maiden he had selected, the old king became sad and said, "You have done ill my son in uncovering what was curtained over. You have placed yourself in great danger. That maiden you selected is in the power of a wicked wizard and kept captive in an iron castle. All who have attempted to set her free have never returned again. But what's done cannot be undone. Your selection is law. Go! Try your luck and may you return home safe and sound!"

The prince took leave of his father, mounted his horse, and rode away in search of his chosen bride. It came to pass that he rode through a vast forest, through which he traveled until the road ended. As he was wandering with his horse in thickets and among rocks and morasses, not knowing which way to turn, he heard some boy shout behind him, "Hi! Stop!"

The prince looked around and saw a tall man hurrying after him. "Stop and take me with you. Take me into your service. You will not regret it!"

"Who are you?" asked the prince. "What can you do?"

"My name is Long and I can extend myself. Do you see a bird's nest in the pine tree? I will bring you the nest down without having to climb up the tree." Long's body grew rapidly until it was as tall as the pine. He then reached the nest and in a moment contracted himself again. He gave the nest to the prince, who replied, "You know the business well, but what's the use of birds' nests to me if you can't lead me out of this forest?" asked the prince.

"Ahem! That's an easy matter," said Long. He began to extend himself until he was three times as high as the highest fir tree in the forest. He looked around and called down, "Here! On this side we have the nearest way out of the forest." He then contracted himself, took the prince's horse by the bridle, and before the prince had any idea of it, they were beyond the forest.

Before them was a long and wide plain, beyond which were tall gray rocks. They were like the walls of a large town surrounded by mountains overgrown with forest trees.

"Yonder, sir, goes my comrade!" said Long. He pointed suddenly to the plain. "You should take him along also in your service. I believe he would serve you well."

"Shout for him and call him here so that I may see what he is good for," said the prince.

"It is a little too far, sir," said Long. "He would hardly hear me and it would take a long time before he came because he has a great deal to carry. I'll jump after him instead." Long again extended himself to such a height that his head plunged into the clouds. He made two or three steps, took his comrade by the arm, and placed him before the prince.

He was a short, thickset fellow with a paunch like a sixty-four-gallon cask.

"Who are you?" demanded the prince. "What can you do?"

"My name is Broad, sir. I can widen myself," answered the man, with a deep bow to the prince.

"Give me a sample of your talents," invited the prince.

"Ride quick sir, quick—back into the forest!" cried Broad, as he began to blow himself out.

The prince didn't understand why he needed to ride away, but seeing that Long made all haste to get into the forest, the prince spurred his horse and rode full gallop after him. It was high time that he did ride away, or else Broad would have squashed him, horse and all, as his paunch rapidly grew in all directions. It filled everything everywhere, just as if a mountain had unrolled.

Broad then took himself back in again and returned to his original size. This raised such a wind that the trees in the forest swayed and bent. "You have played me a nice trick," said the prince. "I'll not be able to find such a fellow every day. Come along with us."

The three proceeded together. When they approached the rocks, they met a man who had his eyes bandaged with a handkerchief. "Sir, this is our third comrade," said Long. "You ought to take him also into your service. I'm sure he won't eat his food in vain."

"Who are you?" quizzed the prince. "Why are your eyes bandaged? Can't you see your way?"

"No, sir. Quite the contrary!" the man exclaimed. "It is just because I see too well that I am obliged to bandage my eyes. I see with bandaged eyes just as well as others with unbandaged eyes. If I were to unbandage them, I look everything through and through. When I gaze sharply at anything it catches fire and bursts into flames. What can't burn splits into pieces. For this reason, my name is Sharpsight." He then turned to a rock opposite him, removed the bandage from his eyes and fixed his flaming gaze on it. The rock began to crackle. Pieces flew on every side, and in a very short time, nothing of it remained but a heap of sand on which something glittered like fire. Sharpsight went to fetch it and brought it to the prince. It was pure gold.

"Heigh-ho! You are a fellow that money can't purchase!" chuckled the prince. "He is a fool who wouldn't make use of your services. If you have such good sight, look and tell me whether it is far to the iron castle. What is happening there now?"

"If you rode by yourself sir," answered Sharpsight, "maybe you wouldn't be able to get there within a year. With us, you will arrive today. They are just getting supper ready for us."

"What is my future bride doing?" asked the prince.

"An iron lattice is before her,
In a tower that's high,
She doth sit and sigh,
A wizard watch and ward keeps o'er her."

The prince cried, "Whoever wants to help me set her free?"

The three men all promised to help him. They guided him among the gray rocks through the breadth that Sharpsight had made in them with his eyes, and farther and farther on, through rocks, high mountains, and deep forests. Whenever there was any obstacle in the road, it was removed by the three comrades.

When the sun was lowering in the west, the mountains became smaller, the forests less dense, and the rocks concealed themselves among the heath. When the sun was almost on the point of setting, the prince saw not far before him an iron castle. At sunset, he rode by an iron bridge to the gate. As soon as the sun went down, the iron bridge rose up and, with a single movement, the gate closed. The prince and his companions were captives in the iron castle.

After they had looked around the courtyard, the prince put his horse up in the stable where everything was ready for it, and they went into the castle. In the court, in the stable, in the castle hall, and in rooms, they saw in the twilight many richly dressed people. They were gentlemen and servants, but not one of them moved—they were all turned to stone.

They went through several rooms and came into the large, brilliantly lit banquet hall. In the middle of the room was a table piled high with

plenty of good meats and drinks. There were places laid out for four people. They waited and waited, thinking that someone would come. When
no one arrived, they finally sat down and ate and drank whatever pleased
them to taste.

When they had finished eating, they looked about to find where they
might sleep. All at once, the door flew open unexpectedly, and into the
room came the wizard. He was a bent old man in a long black outfit with
a bald head, a gray beard down to his knees, and three iron hoops around
his waist. He led by the hand a very beautiful maiden, dressed in white.
She had a silver girdle around her waist and a crown of pearls on her head.
She was pale and sad, as if she had risen from the grave.

The prince recognized her at once, and sprang forward to meet her. Before he could utter a word, the wizard addressed him, "I know why you
have come. You want to take the princess away. Well! So be it. Take her
if you can keep her in sight for three nights so that she doesn't vanish from
you. If she vanishes, you will be turned into stone, as well as your three
servants, just like everyone who has come before you." He then motioned
the princess to a seat and departed.

The prince could not take his eyes off the beautiful princess. He began
to talk to her and asked her all manner of questions, but she neither answered nor smiled. In fact, she never looked at anyone. It seemed that she
was also made of marble.

The prince sat down beside her and vowed that he would not sleep all
night long lest she should vanish from him. Also to ensure that she did
not disappear, Long extended himself like a strap and wound himself
round the whole room along the wall. Broad swelled himself up in the
doorway, and stopped the door up so tight that not even a mouse could
have slipped through. Sharpsight placed himself against a pillar in the
midst of the room and kept watch. Try as hard as they might, they all
began to nod and finally fell asleep. They slept the whole night, just as if
the wizard had thrown them into the water.

When morning began to dawn, the prince was the first to wake. As if a
knife had been thrust into his heart—he realized the princess was gone!
He immediately woke his comrades and asked them what was to be done.

"Never mind, sir," said Sharpsight. He looked intensely out through
the window. "I see her already. A hundred miles away is a forest. In the
midst of the forest is an old oak tree and on top of the oak is an acorn. She
is in that acorn."

Long immediately took Sharpsight on his shoulders, extended himself,
and with Sharpsight showing him the way, traveled ten miles with each
step. No more time had elapsed than would have been needed to move

once around a cottage before they were back again. Long delivered the acorn to the prince. "Let it fall on the ground, sir."

The prince let it fall, and immediately the princess stood beside him. When the sun began to show itself beyond the mountains, the folding doors flew open with a crash and the wizard entered the room smiling spitefully. When he saw the princess he frowned, growled, and with a bang, one of the iron hoops he wore splintered and sprang off of him. He then took the maiden by the hand and led her away.

The whole day after that, the prince had nothing to do but walk up and down the castle, exploring the wonderful things there. Everywhere he looked, it appeared as though life had been lost in a single moment. In one hall, he saw a prince who held in both hands a brandished sword, as if he intended to cleave somebody in two. The blow never fell because he had been turned into stone.

In one chamber was a knight frozen in stone, just as if he had been fleeing from someone in terror and stumbled on the threshold. He was started in a downward direction, but had not fallen. Under the chimney sat a servant who held in one hand a piece of roast meat. Another handful of the meat was suspended in stone before his open mouth.

Many others had been frozen in the exact position they were when the wizard declared, "Be turned into stone."

The prince saw many fine horses, also turned to stone. In the castle and all around, he saw desolation and death. There were trees with no leaves, meadows with no grass, and a river that did not flow. Nowhere was there even a singing bird, or a flower with new buds on the ground, or a white fish in the water.

Morning, noon, and evening, the prince and his companions found good and abundant entertainment in the castle. Wine poured itself. After supper, the folding doors opened again and the wizard brought in the princess for the prince to guard. Although they all determined to exert themselves with all their might not to fall asleep, it was of no use. Fall asleep again they did!

When the prince awoke at dawn and saw that the princess had vanished, he jumped up and pulled Sharpsight by the arm. "Hey! Get up, Sharpsight. Do you know where the princess is?"

He rubbed his eyes, looked, and said, "I see her. There's a mountain two hundred miles off and in the mountain is a rock. In the rock is a precious stone. She's that precious stone. If Long carries me there, we shall rescue her," said Sharpsight.

Long took Sharpsight at once on his shoulders, extended himself, and went twenty miles with each step. Sharpsight fixed his flaming eyes on the mountain. When the mountain crumbled, the rock split into a thousand pieces and among them glittered the precious stone. They took up the stone and brought it to the prince.

When he let it fall on the ground, the princess again stood beside him. Afterward, when the wizard came and saw her there, his eyes flashed with spite and with another bang, an iron hoop cracked upon him and flew off. He growled and led the princess out of the room.

That day, everything was as it had been the day before. After supper, the wizard brought the princess in again. This time, he looked the prince squarely in the face and scornfully uttered the words, "It will be seen who's a match for whom. We will see who is victorious—you or I." After he said this, he turned and left the room.

That night, they all exerted themselves even more to avoid going to sleep. They didn't even sit down. They decided to walk about all night long, but their efforts were in vain. They were bewitched. One fell asleep after the other in their footsteps, and the princess vanished.

In the morning, the prince again woke first. When he didn't see the princess, he woke Sharpsight. "Hey! Get up, Sharpsight! Where is the princess?"

Sharpsight looked for a long time. "Oh, sir," he said. "She is a long way off, a long way off! Three hundred miles off is a black sea, and in the midst of the sea is a shell on the bottom, and in the shell is a gold ring. She is the gold ring. But never mind! We will get her. Today though, Long must take Broad with him as well. We will need him."

Long took Sharpsight on one shoulder and Broad on the other. He went thirty miles with each step. When they came to the black sea, Sharpsight showed Long where he must reach into the water for the shell. Long extended his hand as far as he could, but still could not reach the bottom.

"Wait comrades! Wait just a little and I'll help you," said Broad. He swelled himself out as far as his paunch would stretch. He then lay down on the shore and drank. In a very short time, the water fell so low that Long easily reached the bottom and took the shell out of the sea. From the shell he extracted the ring. He then took his comrades on his shoulders and hurried back. On the way, however, he found it a little difficult to run with Broad, who had half a sea of water inside him, so he took him from his shoulder onto the ground in a wide valley. Thump he went, like a sack let fall from a tower. In a moment, the whole valley was underwater like a vast lake. Broad himself barely crawled out of it.

Meanwhile, the prince was in great trouble in the castle. The dawn began to display itself over the mountains and his servants had not returned. The more brilliantly the rays of the sun ascended, the greater was his anxiety. A heavy perspiration came out on his forehead. Soon the sun showed itself in the east like a thick slip of flame. Then, with a loud crash the door flew open, and on the threshold stood the wizard. He looked around and seeing that the princess was not there, laughed hatefully and stepped into the room.

Suddenly there was a pop, the window flew into pieces, and the gold ring fell on the floor. In an instant, the princess stood by the prince's side. Sharpsight, who had seen what was going on in the castle, told Long that the prince was in danger. Long then had taken a step and thrown the ring through the window into the room.

The wizard roared with rage until the castle quaked and then the third iron hoop that was around his waist sprang off him with a bang. The wizard turned into a raven and flew out and away through the shattered window.

Only then did the beautiful maiden speak and thank the prince for setting her free. She blushed like a rose. In and around the castle, everything became alive once more. The fellow in the hall who was holding the outstretched sword swung it into the air. It whistled and then returned to its sheath. The lad who was stumbling on the threshold, fell on the ground. He immediately got up again and felt his nose to see whether it was still intact. The man who was sitting under the chimney put the piece of meat into his mouth and went on eating. Everybody completed what he had been doing from the point where he had left off.

In the stables, the horses merrily stamped and snorted. The trees around the castle became green like periwinkles, the meadows were full of variegated flowers, and high in the air warbled the skylark. In the clear river, an abundance of small fishes appeared. Everywhere there was life and enjoyment.

Meanwhile, a number of gentlemen gathered in the room where the prince was. All of them thanked him for their liberation. The prince told them, "You have nothing to thank me for. If it had not been for my trusty comrades—Long, Broad, and Sharpsight—I too would have been what you were."

The prince then started immediately on his way home to his father, with his bride and companions. The old king wept for joy at his son's success, for he had feared he would never see him again. Soon afterward, there was a grand wedding. The festivities lasted three weeks. All the gentlemen that the prince had liberated were invited. After the wedding, Long, Broad, and Sharpsight announced to the young king that they were going to leave and go into the world to look for work.

He tried to persuade them to stay with him. "I will give you everything you want as long as you live," he promised them. "You needn't work at all." But they didn't like such an idle life, so they took leave of the young king and his new wife. They left and have been knocking about some-where or other in the world ever since.

Thoughts About the Stories, Discussions, and Activities

THE LION AND THE MOUSE

This is a fable about the rewards of cooperation as demonstrated by two unlikely characters.

- ⊙ *In this story, a large and powerful lion is aided by a tiny mouse. How can those who are often presumed unimportant or weak make a difference to the rich and mighty? Rewrite this fable using human characters in a similar scenario.*
- ⊙ *Have you ever helped someone who was stronger or older than you? Has someone smaller or younger ever helped you? Discuss these instances with others.*

LESSONS FROM A FATHER

This is a wonderful story that shows us why families need to stick together.

- ⊙ *Re-create the demonstration that the father gave his children. Gather a bundle of small twigs and try breaking it. Then try breaking the twigs individually. Discuss what this exercise symbolizes.*

THE HUNT

This is yet another story about a group sticking together for its very own survival.

- ⊙ *Why do you suppose many animals travel in herds or in packs? In the library or on the Internet, research herding or pack animals and write a report on your findings.*
- ⊙ *What is the difference between herds and packs? Discuss whether humans are more like the former or the latter.*

THE ESCAPE OF THE PIGEONS

This story shows how even those captured and in danger can survive if they all pull together.

- ⊙ *The pigeons in this tale freed themselves through cooperation. Throughout history, human beings have done the same. Research examples of cooperation that made change, such as strikes, peace demonstrations, and boycotts. Share your findings in an oral or written report.*

THE GREAT CANOE

This is a story about showing respect for the world around us—and about the great and the small.

- ⊙ *In this story, a community of creatures defends the environment against a misguided human. Do you know of any ways that the environment "tells" us when we are abusing it? Make a list, then write about one of the ways using a folktale format.*
- ⊙ *Rata was rewarded for his eventual cooperation with the forest community. Do you think the environment rewards us when we use its resources responsibly? Discuss your thoughts with others.*

STEALING FIRE

This story gives us another explanation of how creatures pulling together in a spirit of cooperation can provide aid and comfort for all.

- ⊙ *Compare this story with the Paiute version of bringing fire told in "The Sage Grouse." How are they alike? How are they different?*
- ⊙ *How does this story demonstrate cooperation? What other lessons can you find in the story?*

THE CRANE AND THE WOOD GROUSE

This little story from Finland combines the theme of cooperation between the crane and the smaller birds with the common Finnish theme of
forest preservation.

⊙ *This story shows how the forest provides for its creatures. In the library or on the Internet, research the crane and the wood grouse, and
compare your findings to the depictions in this story.*

LONG, BROAD, AND SHARPSIGHT

Success develops when everyone uses their unique differences together
to achieve a common goal.

⊙ *Each of the characters in this story has unique strengths. What are
your strengths and how can they contribute to group success? Make a
list and discuss your thoughts with others.*
⊙ *This story contains many symbols. How many can you find and what
do they represent?*

Other Activity Ideas

⊙ *Here is a passage from Rudyard Kipling's* Second Jungle
Book:

*Now this is the Law of the Jungle—as old and as true as the sky,
and the wolf that shall keep it may prosper. But the wolf that
shall break it must die. As the creeper that girdles the tree trunk,
the law runneth forward and back, for the strength of the pack is
the wolf, and the strength of the wolf is the pack.*

⊙ *Discuss what this quote has to say about cooperation. Research wolves and write a report about wolf behavior.*
⊙ *Interview people about their thoughts on cooperation, then
list all the positive and negative results.*
⊙ *Discuss how you can encourage cooperation in others
around you.*
⊙ *Read the newspaper for one day and make a list of all the examples you can find of cooperation in local, national, and
world events.*

See the "General Activities" section at the back of this book
for more ideas to further explore these topics.

Respect

Intelligence and Luck
(Slavonic)

Once upon a time, Luck met Intelligence on a garden seat. "Make room for me!" demanded Luck. Intelligence was inexperienced at that time and didn't know who ought to make room for whom.

Intelligence said, "Why should I make room for you? You are no better than I."

"He's the better man," answered Luck, "who performs most. See you the peasant's son who is ploughing in the field? Enter into him, and if he gets on better through you than through me, I will always make way submissively for you whenever and wherever we meet."

Intelligence agreed and entered at once into the ploughboy's head. As soon as the ploughboy felt that he had intelligence in his head, he began to think, "Why must I follow the plough to the day of my death? I can go somewhere else and make my fortune more easily." He stopped working, put the plough away, and drove home.

"Father," he said, "I don't like this peasant's life. I would rather learn to be a gardener."

"What ails you Vanek?" his father asked. "Have you lost your wits?" However, after thinking it over, he said, "Well, if you will, learn, and my blessings go with you. Your brother will be heir to the cottage after me."

Vanek didn't care that he lost the cottage. He left, and became apprentice to the king's gardener. For every little thing that the gardener showed him, Vanek comprehended ever so much more. Before long, he didn't even obey the gardener's orders, but did everything his own way.

At first the gardener was angry, but seeing that everything got along better, he was content. "I see that you are more intelligent than I am," said the gardener. Thereafter, he let Vanek garden as he saw fit. In no space of time, Vanek made the garden so beautiful that the king took great delight in it. He frequently walked in the garden with his queen and their only daughter.

The princess was a very beautiful maiden. However, no one had heard a single word from her since she ceased speaking at twelve years old. This grieved the king, and he issued a proclamation that whoever could get the princess to speak again should be her husband.

Many young kings, princes, and other great lords came one after another, but all went away just as they had come. No one succeeded in causing her to speak.

"Why shouldn't I try my luck?" thought Vanek. "Who knows whether I might succeed in bringing her to answer when I ask her a question?" He at once asked to be announced at the palace. The king and his advisors conducted him into the room where the princess was.

The princess had a pretty little dog and was very fond of him because he amused her so much. The dog seemed to understand everything the princess wanted.

When Vanek went into the room with the king and his advisors, he acted as if he didn't even see the princess, but turned to the dog and said, "I have heard little dog, that you are very clever and I have come to you for advice. We are three companions in travel: a sculptor, a tailor, and myself. Once upon a time we were going through a forest and were obliged to pass the night in it. To be safe from wolves, we made a fire and agreed to keep watch one after the other.

"The sculptor kept watch first and for amusement to kill time took a log and carved a lovely maiden out of it. When it was finished, he woke the tailor to keep his turn at the watch. The tailor, seeing the wooden maiden asked what it meant.

"'As you see,' said the sculptor, 'I was weary and didn't know what to do with myself so I carved a fair maiden out of a log. If you find that time is hanging heavy on your hands, you can dress her.'

"The tailor at once took out his scissors, needle, and thread, cut out the clothes, stitched away, and when they were ready, dressed the maiden in the clothes he had made. He then called me to come and keep my turn at watch.

"I also asked him the meaning of what I saw before me. 'As you see,' said the tailor, 'the sculptor found time hanging heavy on his hands and carved the lovely maiden out of a log. I for the same reason clothed her. If you find time hanging heavy on your hands, you can teach her to speak.'

"By morning dawn, I had actually taught her to speak. In the morning, when my companions woke up, each wanted to possess the maiden. The sculptor said, 'I made her.'

"The tailor replied, 'I clothed her.'

"I also maintained my right. Tell me, therefore dear dog, to which of us the maiden belongs."

The dog, of course said nothing. Instead, the princess replied, "To whom can she belong but to yourself? What's the good of the sculptor's maiden without life? What good is the tailor's dressing without speech? There, by rights she belongs to you."

"You have passed your own sentence," said Vanek. "I have given you speech again and a new life. You therefore by rights belong to me."

One of the king's advisors said, "The king will give you rich rewards for succeeding in unloosing his daughter's tongue. You cannot have her to wife since you are of low lineage."

The king said, "You are a gardener. I will give you riches instead of our daughter."

Vanek wouldn't hear of any other reward and said, "The king promised without any exception that whoever caused his daughter to speak again should be her husband. A king's word is law. If the king wants others to observe his laws, he must first keep them himself. Therefore the king *must* give me his daughter."

"Seize and bind him!" shouted one of the king's advisors. "Whoever says the king *must* do anything offers an insult to him. Such a person is worthy of death. May it please you, our king, to order this malefactor to be executed with the sword?"

The king breathed heavily and said, "Let him be executed." Vanek was immediately tied up and led away. When they reached the place of execution, Luck was waiting for him there.

Luck said secretly to Intelligence, "See how this man has got on through you until he has to lose his head! Make way and let me take your place!" As soon as Luck entered Vanek, the executioner's sword broke against the scaffold, just as if someone had snapped it. Before they brought the executioner another, a trumpeter on horseback came galloping as swift as a bird from the city. He trumpeted merrily and waved a white flag. After him came the royal carriage for Vanek.

The princess had told her father that Vanek had spoken the truth and that the king's word ought not to be broken. Even if Vanek were of low lineage, the king could easily make him a prince. The king said, "You are right! Let him be a prince." The royal carriage was immediately sent for Vanek and the advisor who had irritated the king against Vanek was executed in his place.

After the wedding, when Vanek and the princess were riding together in a carriage, Intelligence happened to be somewhere on the road. Seeing that he couldn't avoid meeting Luck, he bent his head and slipped to one side, just as if cold water had been thrown upon him. From that time forth, it is said that Intelligence has always given a wide berth to Luck whenever he has had to meet him.

Healing Well
(Scotland)

A healing well is part of a Scottish story on Islay.

One day, the queen fell ill and told her oldest daughter to go to the Well of True Water and bring her a drink. She was sure this would restore her health. At the well, a large frog approached the princess and asked her to marry him. She was offended and refused. The frog then denied her water from the well.

When she returned home with no water, the queen sent her younger sister to the well instead, but the same thing happened to her. Feeling sicker and sicker, the queen finally sent her youngest daughter to the well. Again, the frog appeared and asked the young maiden to marry him.

When she realized that this was the only way she could get water, she agreed. She took the water to her mother and it healed her. That night, the frog came to their dwelling and asked the princess to take him to her bedchamber. Next, he told her to end his torture by cutting off his head. When she did, the frog was transformed into a handsome young man. He was the son of a king who had been under a spell, and she had saved his life by agreeing to marry him.

And, of course, they all lived happily ever after.

Two Friends
(Africa)

In deepest, darkest Africa, there was a time when Frog and Snake were friends. Frog, who usually stayed near the water where he was born, discovered Snake one day when he was hopping down a path. He had never seen anything like this creature before. Snake looked almost like a stick, but stretched across the path in several curves with a skin that gleamed many colors in the sunlight.

"What are you? I have never seen you before. What are you doing on the path? An animal might step on you and hurt you," Frog said quickly.

"Hello little hopping thing. I am Snake, and the reason I am on the path is that it is so warm here in this spot of sunlight. Who are you?" replied Snake. As he spoke, he moved his body slowly from curves to a sticklike form, and then back again into new curves.

"I am Frog," was the answer. "Let's play together."

For the rest of the warm morning they played together, showing each other tricks they could do. "Can you do this?" asked Frog, as he hopped in a circle and landed right in front of Snake's head.

"No," was Snake's answer. "I can't do that, but watch what I can do." Snake slithered over to a tree along the path, crawled up the tree, wrapped himself around a branch, and traveled out onto its very tip.

The two new friends were delighted with what the other could do and tried to create new things that they could do to please each other. When it turned into late afternoon, Frog said, "I must go home now, Snake. I am hungry and must get home before dark."

"Let's meet here again tomorrow," suggested Snake. "We can play together again."

"Yes, that would be pleasant," answered Frog. "I have enjoyed watching you move and showing me things I have never seen before. I will see you in the morning."

Frog went home to his family. As they were eating, he told his mother about the new friend he had played with that day. "He looked so pretty in the sun as he slid up the tree and coiled himself around a branch, mother."

"Who is this new friend?" Frog's mother asked him.

"He called himself Snake," Frog answered.

"Dear child, don't you know you were in danger? Snakes are our enemies. Promise me you won't ever play with Snake again. He could harm you," his mother instructed him firmly.

While Frog and his mother were talking, Snake had gone home to his family. "Guess who I played with today? Guess what he can do?" Snake told his mother.

"Who was this and what could they do?" she asked.

"He was called Frog, and he could hop in the air, land, and hop more times. He was such fun to watch and be with," Snake said gleefully.

"Oh, child of mine," mother snake told her child, "Frogs are not friends of ours. They are food for us. If you ever see one again, catch it and eat it. They are delicious."

The very next morning, Frog and Snake met on the path again. "I can't play with you anymore," Frog told Snake. "My mother warned me that I am in danger with you," he said, and hopped back away from Snake.

Snake also remembered what his mother had told him. "My mother says that frogs are delicious meals for us. In spite of that, I really enjoyed playing with you yesterday."

Life was lonely after that for both Snake and Frog. They never played together or talked with each other. Their one day of playing and friendship was never to be again.

The Man Who Roared
(Colorado, USA)

One spring day, in a little village high on a southern Colorado mountainside, a group of children were playing in the fields to the north of town. Years later, one of them, whose name was Peter, first told the story of what happened that afternoon. His story is still told around the village fireplaces when the wind is blowing loud and cold through the trees of the valley where Peter lived.

On that sunny afternoon so long ago, Peter and his playmates had started several games, but rapidly tired of each and then started playing something else—it was that sort of a day. The sun was high and although it was still cool in the shade, it was uncomfortably warm in the direct sun. The fields where Peter and his friends played were covered with sharp hay stubble and many hidden rocks that could quite easily trip one up.

The children continued playing, shouting, and running around pell-mell. They had been forbidden by their parents to go to these fields, and knew that they would undoubtedly be told to return and play in the village square, the plaza, by the first adult who saw them. But, no one came along.

In time, their excitement over all their adventures died down, their voices became less shrill, and several of them wished that someone would come along and send them back. Playing where they were forbidden wasn't half the fun they had thought it would be. Then, a grown man came in sight, walking down the trail that passed through the fields where they played. The moment the youngsters saw him, they stopped what they were doing and stood silently watching this strange man.

The children noticed that the man was coming down the trail, not up from the village. They wondered who would be up on the mountaintop at this time of the year. It was not yet true summer and the wind higher up was harsh and filled with the bite of the snow that still covered the entire upper half of the high, huge mountain.

The young folk watchfully stared at the man, but he did not seem to notice them. If he did, they weren't able to tell, for he never looked their way. He just continued walking down the rocky trail. Then, for no apparent reason, one of the children laughed, then another, and another. The children were being very rude. Their parents had certainly taught them better, but they were playing on forbidden fields and didn't care what they did. One of them pointed out, "Look at that funny man!"

He was dressed all right, looked all right, and walked all right. Everything about him was all right; that is, everything but his hat. It was his hat that made him seem such a funny man to them. The stranger was wearing one of those felt, flat-crowned hats with little balls of yarn hung all around the brim. "Where did you get that hat?" yelled one of the boys. "At a circus or a carnival?"

Then, as suddenly as water rushes from a broken dam, they all ran toward him, laughing and jeering at the man and his hat. He stopped abruptly and looked up at the children with perplexed eyes. When he stopped walking and stood looking at them, the children stopped laughing. "He won't harm us," said one of the bigger boys. And again the wild, rude children started jeering.

The man with the hat stood a moment and looked at them, then he turned and without a word, walked on down the trail just a bit quicker than he had walked before.

One of the boys, who himself had been teased regularly by the others, called out a few words to the man. A girl ran in close and tried to spit on him, or at least she made spitting noises. Then, one of the youngest among them picked up a pebble and shied it at the man, but it missed and clattered on down the hillside.

Before anyone knew what was happening, they were all throwing rocks. Few of them hit the man, but some did find their mark. Slowly, the man stopped and turned toward the youngsters. They were all expecting him to shout at them, but to their surprise, he roared. He roared a roar that was heard seven miles away by men from the village who were cutting piñon wood.

The young ones stopped in their tracks and immediately ceased throwing rocks. Those who still held some in their hands tried to drop them behind their backs so the man would not see. They all stood silent and then the man roared again. Later, one man of the village who had heard the roar from miles away said, "That sounds exactly like a lion I once heard in a circus."

Upon hearing the second roar, the youngsters all ran madly away from the roaring man. He picked up a handful of pebbles and started to throw them at the running children, missing most of them.

The children ran to the safety of a nearby abandoned shed of logs. They cowered there for four long hours, while rocks, earth, sticks, and even pinecones showered down upon the roof. As time passed, of course, the children no longer thought the man was funny. They feared that they would be buried alive in the shed by the amount of sticks and rocks and such the man was throwing. Then they heard unusually loud falling rocks, followed by one gigantic sounding rock and everything became suddenly quiet.

Inside the cabin, no one dared to move. They didn't even think to look out and see if they had been covered over by rocks and sticks. Finally, when one of them peeked through a narrow crack in the heavy door of the shed, he shouted loudly and jerked the door open. There was nothing on the roof or lying on the earth near the shed. No rocks, no sticks, no pinecones or clods of dirt. There was nothing to be seen but the barren, trampled ground that many animals had walked over.

Later, many people in the village shook their heads in bewilderment over the children's story. Had it not been for the woodcutters, who clearly heard the two great lionlike roars, they would have thought that the children made up the entire tale just to cover up the fact that they had been playing in forbidden territory.

Today, Peter's story is still told to the grandchildren of the elders who had once, a long time ago, been part of a group of rude children who saw a man who roared.

Thoughts About the Stories, Discussions, and Activities

INTELLIGENCE AND LUCK

This is a story of a contest between Intelligence and Luck. Which is more important?

- ⊙ *Do you respect times when luck and intelligence are needed to achieve your goals? Can you remember any times in your life when intelligence or luck helped you? Write a story about such a time.*

HEALING WELL

This is a variant of the Frog Prince story.

- ⊙ *What does this story have to say about judging others on their appearances, station in life, or wealth? Discuss what it teaches us about respect.*

TWO FRIENDS

In this tale, we see an example of how two friends are labeled by others. Their friendship becomes something that neither of them is essentially allowed.

⊙ *Children often exhibit more tolerance and respect for others than their parents. Can you think of any instances of this in contemporary society? Discuss some examples.*

⊙ *What is the difference between tolerance and acceptance? One person defined tolerance as "one must put up with another person's differences." Another defined acceptance as "celebrating these differences." List other definitions, and give examples of how we can focus on our commonalities rather than our differences.*

THE MAN WHO ROARED

This legend explores the gang mentality of bullies that takes over even among otherwise nice people. Someone who is different always seems to be the object of the bullies.

⊙ *In daily school situations, have you ever observed personal attacks among people? Establish a discussion group to share thoughts about cliques, discrimination, and the pain of being picked on. After discussion, plan an activity to address these concerns in a positive way.*

Other Activity Ideas

- Research concepts and customs of different cultures, past and present, to use in discussing respect. For instance, in Celtic mythology, salmon and trout are respected because they are linked to sacred wells and springs, places of physical healing, and spiritual rebirth. Salmon are said to eat the hazelnuts that fall into the pool from the tree of knowledge, thereby gaining wisdom and vision, and renewing and sustaining life. In many cultures, respect is shown to the elderly in special ways. What might some of these bits of wisdom have to say about respect, respecting others, and respecting the world around us?

- What does the saying, "Be kind, for everyone you meet is fighting a battle" infer with regard to respect?

- Read other folk stories or books and identify examples of respect or gratitude.

- Discuss how words can hurt others. Make a list of the words that are most disrespectful and hurtful to you. Then list those that are most respectful and nourishing to you.

- Is obesity a legitimate cause for lack of respect? Find and list examples of this form of disrespect in books and in the media. Respect involves lack of discrimination. Does a person's waist size relate to their character?

- Discuss the difference between bias and discrimination.

- ⊙ *Studies have shown that in corporate ladders of success, tall men fare better than short or average men. Explain why you think this is a fact, or why you disagree.*

- ⊙ *Invite a variety of speakers from the community—such as politicians, policemen, or corporate members—to come and address the topic of diversity. One school official said, "You are not going to learn if you don't feel safe and if there is no mutual respect for you and your attitudes." Discuss this statement.*

- ⊙ *Age is another aspect for examining differences. A women's group has incorporated the symbols of red hats and purple dresses as a way to greet middle age.*

    - ⊙ *Where did these symbols come from? (Refer to the poem "Warning" by British writer Jenny Joseph.)*

    - ⊙ *Read material related to this on the Internet. The website www.redhatsociety.org is a good place to start. Share your reactions to these comments with others.*

See the "General Activities" section at the back of this book for more ideas to further explore these topics.

Fairness

The Bagpiper and the Rats
(Germany)

A very long time ago, the town of Hamel in Germany was in-
vaded by bands of rats, the like of which had never been
seen before nor will ever be again. They were great black creatures that boldly ran through the streets in broad daylight and
swarmed all over the houses.

When dressing in the morning, people found them in their
breeches and petticoats, in their pockets, and in their boots.
When they wanted a morsel to eat, the greedy horde would sweep
away everything from cellar to garret. At night, as soon as the
lights were out, these untiring nibblers set to work, making so furious a noise that a deaf man could not have rested for one hour.

Neither cats nor dogs nor poison nor traps would do anything.
The more rats they killed, the more came. One Friday, however,
there arrived in the town a man with a queer face, who played
the bagpipes and sang this refrain:

"Who lives shall see,
Here he is,
The rat catcher."

He was a great, gawky fellow, dry and bronzed, with a crooked
nose, a long rat-tail mustache, and two large yellow piercing and
mocking eyes under a big felt hat with a scarlet cock's feather. He
was dressed in a green jacket with a leather belt and red breeches.
On his feet were sandals fastened by thongs passed around his legs.

That is how he may be seen to this day, painted on a window of the Hamel cathedral.

He stopped on the great marketplace before the town hall, turned his back to the church, and went on with his music. The town council had just assembled to consider once more this plague of Egypt. The stranger sent word to the counselors that if they would make it worth his while, he would rid them of all their rats before nightfall.

"Then he is a sorcerer!" cried the citizens with one voice. "We must beware of him."

But the town counselor, who was considered clever, said, "Sorcerer or no, if this bagpiper speaks the truth, it was he who sent us this horrible vermin that he wants to rid us of today for money. Well, we must learn to catch the devil in his own snares. You just leave it to me."

"Leave it to the town counselor," said the citizens one to another. And the stranger was brought before them.

"Before night," said he, "I shall have dispatched all the rats in Hamel if you will pay me a gros a head."

"A gros a head!" cried the citizens, "but that will come to millions of florins!"

The town counselor simply shrugged his shoulders and said to the stranger, "A bargain! To work! You will be paid one gros a head as you ask."

The bagpiper announced that when the moon rose that evening, the inhabitants should leave the streets free and content themselves with looking out of their windows.

Toward nine o'clock that night, the bagpiper appeared on the marketplace. As he had done earlier, he turned his back to the church, and the moment the moon rose on the horizon, "Trarira, trari!" the bagpipes resounded.

At first it was a slow, caressing sound, then more and more lively and urgent. It penetrated the farthest alleys of the town. Soon, from the bottom of the cellars, the top of the garrets, from under all the furniture, from all the nooks and corners of the houses, out came the rats and they began to run toward the front of the town hall. They were so squeezed together that they covered the pavement. When the square was quite full, the bagpiper faced about, and still playing briskly, turned toward the river that runs at the foot of the walls of Hamel.

When he got to the river, he turned around. The rats were following. "Hop! Hop!" he cried, pointing with his finger to the middle of the stream, where the water whirled and was drawn down as if through a funnel. "Hop! Hop!" Without hesitating, the rats took the leap, swam straight to the funnel, plunged in head foremost, and disappeared.

The plunging continued without ceasing until midnight. At last, dragging himself with difficulty, came a big rat, white with age, that stopped on the bank. This was the king of the rat band.

"Are they all there, friend Blanchet?" asked the bagpiper.

"They are all there," replied Blanchet.

"And how many were they?"

"Nine hundred and ninety thousand, nine hundred and ninety-nine."

"Well reckoned?"

"Well reckoned."

"Then go and join them, old sire. Au Revoir." The old white rat sprang in his turn into the river and swam to the whirlpool where he disappeared.

When the bagpiper had thus concluded his business, he went to bed at his inn. For the first time in three months, the people of Hamel slept quietly through the night. The next morning at nine o'clock, the bagpiper repaired to the town hall where the town council awaited him.

"All your rats took a jump into the river yesterday," said he to the counselors. "I guarantee that not one of them comes back. They were nine hundred and ninety thousand, nine hundred and ninety-nine, at one gros a head. Reckon!"

"Let us reckon the heads first. One gros a head is one head the gros. Where are the heads?"

The rat catcher did not expect this treacherous stroke. He paled with anger and his eyes flashed fire. "The heads!" cried he. "If you care about them, go and find them in the river."

"So," replied the town counselor, "you refuse to hold to the terms of your agreement? We ourselves could refuse you all payment. But you have been of use to us and we will not let you go without reward," and he offered him fifty crowns.

"Keep your reward for yourself," replied the rat catcher proudly. "If you do not pay me, I will be paid by your heirs." Thereupon, he pulled his hat down over his eyes, went out of the hall, and left town without speaking to a soul.

When the people of Hamel heard how the affair had ended, they rubbed their hands and laughed over the rat catcher, who, they said, was caught in his own trap. The next day, which was a Sunday, they all went gaily to church, never suspecting the terrible surprise that awaited them on their return home. There were no children anywhere. They had all disappeared! "Our children! Where are our poor children?" was soon the cry in all the streets.

Then, through the east door of the town came three little boys, who cried and wept, and this is what they told. While the parents were at church, a wonderful music had resounded. Soon, all the little boys and girls that had been left at home came out, attracted by the magic sounds, and had rushed to the great marketplace. There they found the rat catcher playing his bagpipes in the same spot as the evening before. Then the stranger had begun to walk quickly and they had followed, running, singing, and dancing to the sound of the music. They traveled as far as the foot of the mountain that one sees on entering Hamel.

At their approach, the mountain had opened a little, and the bagpiper went in with the children. The mountain closed again after them. Only the three little ones who told the adventure had remained outside, as if by a miracle. One was bandy-legged and could not run fast enough. Another, who had left the house in haste—one foot shod, the other bare—had hurt himself against a big stone and could not walk without difficulty. The third had arrived in time, but in hurrying to go in with the others had struck so violently against the wall of the mountain that he fell backward at the moment it closed upon his comrades.

Hearing the boys' story, the parents redoubled their lamentations. They ran with their pikes and mattocks to the mountain and searched until evening for the opening through which their children had disappeared. They were not able to find it. At last, the night falling, they returned to Hamel in desolation.

But, the unhappiest of all was the town counselor, for he had lost three little boys and two pretty little girls.

What had become of all these unfortunate children?

The parents always hoped that they were not dead and that the rat catcher had taken them with him to his country. For several years, they went in search of them to different countries, but no one ever came on the trace of the poor little ones. It was not until much later that anything was heard of them.

About 150 years after the event, when there was no longer one left of the fathers, mothers, brothers, or sisters of that day, there arrived one evening in Hamel some merchants of Bremen returning from the East, who asked to speak with the citizens.

They told that in crossing Hungary, they had sojourned in a mountainous country called Transylvania, where the inhabitants spoke only German. In all the places around Transylvania, nothing was spoken but Hungarian. The Transylvanians also declared that they came from Germany, but they did not know how they chanced to be in this strange country. "Now," said the merchants of Bremen, "these Germans cannot be other than the descendants of the lost children of Hamel."

The people of Hamel did not doubt it. Since that day, they regard it as certain that the Transylvanians of Hungary are their country folk.

Coyote and Fox

(Native American, Colorado, USA)

Out in an open field, Coyote chased a mouse from clumps of brush to tall grasses, but he could not catch him. Coyote was skittering around, making sharp turns, when the mouse executed a neat, quick change of direction. Fox was watching all this and shouted, "Ooo-oo-ooo-hoo!" Of course, Coyote found this taunting so upsetting that he became very angry, stopped chasing the mouse, and instead took off after Fox.

Fox was prepared for this, and led Coyote on a frustrating hunt. When Coyote finally caught up with Fox, he was startled to find him standing by a fire. Now, Fox had started the fire, but it was surprising that he started to plead with Coyote not to eat him. "Please don't eat me. We are both in danger from the fire. The only way we can save ourselves is to climb into these two burlap bags."

"Why should I do such a thing?" asked Coyote.

Fox, however, convinced Coyote that they must hurry and save themselves. "Quick, Coyote, get into this sack and I will tie you up and then I will get into the other one and tie the bag up myself. I know how to do this. Hurry! We must save ourselves."

The urgency of Fox's actions convinced Coyote, and he agreed. Fox threw one of the burlap bags over Coyote and tied it up. Then, being wily Fox, he threw the sack into the fire and ran away laughing.

Coyote managed to get out of the bag, but not before he was painfully burned. Now he was really mad. "Just you wait, Fox! I'm going to get you and you will be my supper!"

Coyote followed Fox's trail and found him holding up a huge boulder. "This rock is about to fall on us," panted Fox. "I am getting really tired of holding it up. I need to go get a drink from the lake. You hold it while I am gone so it doesn't fall on us." Before he really thought about it, Coyote put his paws on the boulder, pushed, and waited for Fox to return. The longer he held it, the angrier he got, until Coyote decided he really didn't care if the rock fell or not. He let go of the rock and, of course, it didn't fall. It never budged.

Coyote was furious and took off to find Fox, vowing to make him suffer before he ate him as a succulent supper. Coyote loped off to the lake and just as he thought he would, he found Fox. He was ready to pounce, when Fox said, "I'm sorry, Coyote. Wait, I have been trying to reach the cheese in the water to bring to you. I wanted to make it all up to you and bring you a gift." Fox pointed to the reflection of the moon in the still water of the lake.

By this time, Coyote was quite hungry.

"Climb on the log," Fox told him. "I will push it near the cheese so you can get it."

Coyote did as Fox ordered, and as soon as he reached the end of the log, Fox tipped it over and "splash!" Coyote fell into the lake. If there is one thing that Coyote hates, it is being in water, but even more than that, it is being tricked by Fox over and over again.

Coyote scrambled to the shore, and without even taking the time to shake himself off, he went after Fox. Beside himself with fury, he dug his paw-nails into the ground, once again vowing to do horrible things to his tormentor. Coyote found Fox quietly stirring a stick inside a beehive. Fox was very careful about the way he stirred.

"What are you doing now?" demanded Coyote.

"Shhh! I am teaching school. Can't you hear my students reading?" answered Fox. "I am going to be paid a dozen fat hens for this. Do you want to teach for a while? Because I have sported with you, I'll make it up to you. You teach for a while, and I will go get the fat hens and share them with you."

Greedy Coyote forgot his rage. At that moment, all he could think of was his hunger. He could hear the students reading inside the beehive, so he felt safe. "All right, I'll teach them," Coyote said, and started stirring the beehive with the stick. He was very cautious with his stirring at first, but then he got bored and gave the beehive a whack. The bees boiled out of the hive and stung him everywhere. They swarmed like a cloud around his head and stung him so badly that he could hardly see. Half blind, hurting everywhere, and in a vengeful state of hostility, Coyote kicked up dust as he tore after Fox.

Coyote found him calmly sitting and eating a watermelon. "I am eating half of this watermelon. That way, it won't be so heavy to carry the other half to you," explained Fox. "Of course, I was going to bring your share to you, but since you are here now, why don't you eat your half, Coyote? In fact, Coyote, I'll get another watermelon tomorrow if you will get us another one the next night." Fox sounded so sincere that Coyote agreed.

The watermelon patch belonged to an old couple. When they discovered some watermelons missing, they set up a scarecrow covered with tar. The next night when Fox came, he found the scarecrow and said to it, "Do you think I am afraid of you?" Fox struck the scarecrow with his left paw and when he couldn't get away, he kicked at the scarecrow with his hind feet. Fox was completely stuck.

The old couple found Fox stuck to the scarecrow and they were about to kill him.

"Don't kill me," Fox pleaded. "Coyote has been forcing me to steal. If you let me go and let me take a melon to Coyote, I'll get him to come to your watermelon patch himself tomorrow night." Fox seemed so frightened of Coyote that the old couple agreed and set him free.

Fox returned to Coyote with the melon and bragged as he told him all about the scarecrow. "It caught me, but it was easy to get loose. You won't have any trouble with it tomorrow night."

Coyote went to the patch the next night, and found himself a prisoner of the scarecrow covered with tar. When he smacked the scarecrow to show how cool he was, he got stuck, and then smacked it with his other paw. He couldn't get any of his paws loose; his tail was even plastered tight into the tar. The old couple grabbed Coyote, strung him up on a tree, and skinned him. They left only the hide on top of Coyote's head and on his paws.

"Never come back here again," they warned Coyote, and they let him go.

Coyote decided that since Fox had gotten him into so much trouble, he would never again have anything to do with him. He was done with Fox forever.

Fox was nearby and watched Coyote trotting away. He started to laugh, "Goodbye, Coyote! You look so much better than when I first met you. Look at your handsome toupee and furry gloves." Coyote just kept on walking, wiser but certainly a different-looking animal than when he first started to chase Fox.

Note: Reprinted from *Celebrating the Earth: Stories, Experiences, and Activities* by Norma J. Livo ©2000 Libraries Unlimited.

Toads and Diamonds
(France)

Once upon a time, there was a widow who had two daughters. The older daughter was just like her mother in face and humor, and that wasn't very nice because she was extremely disagreeable, arrogant, and proud. The younger daughter was quite the opposite, just like her father. She was courteous, sweet of temper, and on top of all of that, she was one of the most beautiful girls ever seen.

The widow doted on her older daughter. At the same time, she had a horrible dislike for the younger girl, who was made to eat in the kitchen, away from her mother and sister, and had to work, work, work continually.

One of her chores was to draw water twice daily from a fountain that was a mile and a half away from the house. One day, when the younger daughter was getting water, a poor woman appeared and begged, "Please give me a drink of your water. I am faint with thirst."

"Oh! Of course, you poor thing. Here, refresh yourself," said the pretty little girl. She rinsed out her pitcher and scooped up some water from the clearest place of the fountain. She held up the pitcher for the old woman so that she could drink easier.

After the old woman had drunk, she said, "You are so pretty. Not only are you pretty, but you are good as well. On top of all of that, you are quite mannerly. I cannot help but give you a gift." The old woman was really a fairy who had taken her other form to see just how far the good manners of this pretty girl would go.

"I will give you a special gift. At every word you speak, there shall come out of your mouth either a flower or a jewel."

The pretty little girl curtsied to the fairy and thanked her. When she got home, her mother scolded her, "What kept you so long? What mischief were you getting into? You were only to bring home water!"

"Excuse me mother," said the girl, "for taking so much time." As she said these words, out of her mouth came two roses, two pearls, and two diamonds.

"What is that? What do I see there?" asked the astonished mother. "My eyes may be playing tricks on me, but I think I see pearls and diamonds coming out of your mouth! How can this be?"

As the young girl told her mother all about what had happened, infinite numbers of diamonds fell from her lips.

"Mercy me!" exclaimed the mother. "I must send my darling oldest there. Come quickly, Fanny. Look what is coming out of your sister's mouth when she speaks. You must have the same gift yourself. You only need to go to the fountain, draw water, and when a poor old woman asks you for a drink, give her one quickly."

"Ha! Wouldn't that be a fine sight to see!" sneered Fanny. "Just imagine me, drawing water!"

"You must go at once and don't give me a problem. Go this minute," ordered her mother. Grumbling as she went, Fanny carried the best silver tankard in the house with her. No sooner was she at the fountain than she saw a gloriously dressed lady coming out of the wood. The lady came right up to Fanny and asked, "I would like a drink of your water. Please share some with me."

This was, of course, the same fairy who had given the gift of diamonds and flowers to the younger daughter, but since the elegant lady didn't match the description her sister had given, Fanny was rude. In her proudest tone, she said, "Have I come here to serve you with water? Do you think my silver tankard was brought just for your use? Maybe I will give you a drink and maybe I won't."

"You certainly do not exhibit good manners," answered the fairy. "Since you are of such little breeding and manners, I will give you a special gift. At every word you speak, a snake or a toad will come out of your mouth."

With a shake of her head, Fanny snorted and returned home, still grumbling to herself. When she saw her mother, her mother cried out, "Well, Fanny. Speak to me and let me watch the flowers and diamonds drop from your lips."

"Indeed, mother," answered the arrogant girl. As she said this, out of her mouth came two vipers and two toads.

"Mercy, mercy! What do I see coming from your mouth?" asked her mother. "Your sister must have caused this to happen. She will pay for this!" Immediately the mother ran for the younger daughter, caught her, and beat her. When she was done, the girl fled away and went to hide in the forest.

It happened that the king's son, on his return from hunting, met her there. "My, aren't you the pretty young thing!" he said gently. "What are you doing here alone? Why are you crying?"

"Alas! I have had to escape from my mother and her beating. I have run here for safety," she answered, wiping tears from her eyes. As she said this, the prince saw five or six pearls and as many diamonds come out of her mouth. "Tell me what has happened to you," he said.

With that, the girl told him the whole story. As she talked, and dropped jewels and flowers, the prince fell in love with her. "Dear maiden, you are so sweet and words and jewels from your mouth are so precious, I fear that I am in love with you. Come home to the palace of my father, the king. Let us be married."

That is just exactly what happened. As for her older sister, she was so hateful that finally she turned even her own mother away from her. A miserable wretch, Fanny wandered about for a long time without finding anybody to take her in. She may still be wandering to this very day, grumbling and spewing forth snakes and toads.

Thoughts About the Stories, Discussions, and Activities

THE BAGPIPER AND THE RATS

This tale is a variation on the Pied Piper of Hamlin. In it, the townspeople are not willing to live up to the agreement they had made with the piper. The whole town pays a very high price for their unfairness.

⊚ *Unfair business practices often crop up, even today. Research the newspaper to find current reports of this type of unfair cheating. Share your findings.*
⊚ *Locate Hamel and Transylvania on a map. Do you think this story has any basis in fact? Why or why not?*

COYOTE AND FOX

In this story, one character takes advantage of the other. There is no display of fairness throughout the story.

⊚ *This is a funny story, but the issue of fairness is serious. How can humor help us learn about serious issues? Find other stories to illustrate your point.*

TOADS AND DIAMONDS

This is a variant of the Cinderella story, in which one of the children is misused and mistreated.

- ⊙ *Collect other versions of the Cinderella story. Why did the mother or stepmother not treat each child equally? Discuss whether or not this behavior was fair.*
- ⊙ *In this story, bad behavior is eventually punished. Do you think this is usually the case? Think of your own experiences with unfair situations and write about them.*

Other Activity Ideas

- ⊙ Make a list of times when people have been fair or unfair to you.
- ⊙ Can you find any riddles that relate to fairness? Create your own such riddles and share them with others.
- ⊙ Investigate and make a collection of proverbs about fairness.
- ⊙ What acts that seem unfair to young people seem fair to adults? Why do you think opinions on fairness differ or change?
- ⊙ Compare fairness issues among siblings. How are first-born children treated in comparison to brothers and sisters? Is this fair?
- ⊙ What are the various meanings of "fair"? What are the meanings of "rich"? Write a story developing the concept of fairness organized around "rich."
- ⊙ Tell or write a story titled, "The Fairest Day of My Life." What made that day so fair for you?
- ⊙ Establish a special day, celebration, or event to honor "Fairness." Develop a program of events and activities that could be included in such a celebration.
- ⊙ Have you ever felt that you were treated unfairly? Write a journal entry about the experience, and then rewrite the story with a "fair" ending.
- ⊙ Is fairness the same as justice? Are court decisions fair? Why or why not?

⊙ *Research a famous trial in the library or on the Internet (e.g., the Rosenberg trial, Scopes Monkey trial). Have a class debate on whether or not the verdict and sentence were fair.*

See the "General Activities" section at the back of this book for more ideas to further explore these topics.

Dealing With Bullies

Three Billy Goats Gruff
(Norway)

Long ago, in the far northern country of Norway, three billy goats named Gruff were going up a hillside. They were seeking a pasture rich in grass and other goodies to eat so they could get fat.

Their trip came to a bridge over a swift-running stream. They had to cross over this bridge to get up to the fresh pasture they could see. There was only one problem—a great, ugly troll lived under the bridge. He had a long, sharp nose like a poker and eyes that were dark and as big as saucers. He heard the goats coming and came out from under the bridge.

The youngest billy goat Gruff was the first one to start over the bridge. As he walked on it, you could hear: *Trip trap! Trip trap!*

The troll roared at the little goat, "Who's that tripping over my bridge?"

"Oh, it is only me," said the tiniest billy goat Gruff in a small and shaky voice. "I am on my way up that hillside to get to the rich pasture there. I plan to eat, and eat, and eat, until I get fat."

"Wonderful! Here I come to gobble you up," snarled the troll, as he started to come up to get the little goat.

"Oh no," pleaded the little goat. "Please don't take me. I'm too little to make a good meal for you. Wait a little bit longer and the second billy goat Gruff will be here. He will make a much better meal for you."

"Well, in that case, be off with you," ordered the troll.

Just as the little billy goat Gruff had said, shortly the second billy goat Gruff came up to the bridge and started to cross it. *Trip trap! Trip trap! Trip trap!* went the bridge, as the goat walked on it.

"Who's that tripping over my bridge?" roared the troll.

"Oh, it is just the second billy goat Gruff. I'm going to join my little brother goat and go up to the hillside so I can eat, and eat, and eat until I am fat." His voice didn't show as much fear as the little billy goat Gruff's.

"Ha! I am coming to gobble you up for my meal," announced the troll.

"Oh no, you don't want to take me. Wait a little longer and the big billy goat Gruff will be here. He will make a much better meal, for he is much bigger," said the second billy goat Gruff.

Sure enough, right behind him came the third billy goat Gruff. *Trip trap! Trip trap! Trip trap! Trip trap!* went the bridge when the heavy billy goat started to cross it. The bridge creaked and groaned from under his weight.

"Who's that tramping over my bridge?" roared the troll.

"It is I. I am the big billy goat Gruff," said the largest billy goat, with an ugly, hoarse voice.

"Ha! Now I am coming to gobble you up for my meal," announced the troll.

"Well, then, come along! I have two spears and I will poke your eyeballs out at your ears. Besides, I have two great big stones and I will crush you to bits—body and bones!" taunted the third billy goat Gruff. After saying this, he flew at the troll and poked his eyes out with his horns. He then proceeded to crush him to bits, body and bones, and ended up tossing what was left of the troll out into the stream.

When he was done with that, the largest billy goat Gruff went up the hillside with the other billy goats. The last that was seen of them, the three billy goats had become so fat from eating that they scarcely were able to walk back home. If the fat hasn't left them yet, why, they must still be fat!

Snip, snap, snout,
This tale's told out.

Basket Woman
(Ute, North America)

Cackling old Basket Woman was creeping up on children who were still out after they should have been home. She was a huge ogress, who carried a cane and a basket on her back that was made of woven snakes.

She found a child, whacked it on the head with her cane, and threw it into her basket. She found a second child, thumped it on the head, and tossed it on top of the other child. The third child was harder to catch, but she finally caught him, clobbered him on his head, and flung him into the basket with the others. She really had to sneak up on the fourth child, whacked him on his head, and flipped him into her basket. "That looks like enough children for now," she cackled. Making ferocious noises, she took off for her home up on Ute Mountain.

Before going out to catch children, she had put on a huge pot of water to boil. Now, she had everything she needed for her supper. The pot was boiling and bubbling nicely. She was partial to eating tender children, and was already licking her lips in anticipation.

There was only one problem. Basket Woman didn't know that the father of one of the missing children had discovered his child was gone and started out looking for him. The man had seen Basket Woman as she was sneaking up on the fourth child, so he followed her. This wasn't difficult, since her cackling could be heard clearly throughout the forest as she made her way up to Ute Mountain.

Just as Basket Woman was getting ready to put the children into the boiling pot, the father took off his beaded headband and swung it out at her. When it hit her, she fell into the bubbling hot water and started to shrivel. She melted and disappeared completely.

The children all came back to life and ran home. From then on, they always made sure to get home before it was dark!

The Monkeys and the Grasshoppers
(Hmong, Southeast Asia)

Everyone knows that the grasshoppers were the first living things on earth, but the sky spirit was dissatisfied because it thought the grasshoppers were stupid, so it created humans. Then there were the monkeys. At first man and monkey lived together in friendship, but through the trickery of man, monkeys learned to avoid man. In the jungle, monkeys developed into bullies and they terrorized other creatures that lived there. This is one of those stories.

One day, a group of monkeys came upon the body of a dead monkey in the jungle. They gathered around the body and could see that he had been killed. "Who killed our cousin?" they cried. This question was followed by much discussion and argument. "I know, it must have been the grasshoppers!" one of them declared.

"Yes, yes, that it is!" they shouted. The group planned their revenge on the grasshoppers. "In the morning we must go up to the grasshopper hill and fight them for killing our cousin," became the battle cry.

Early the next morning, the monkeys swept up the hill with the intent of wreaking havoc. "Look out grasshoppers!" they roared. "We are going to fight you for killing our cousin!" This was the message the monkeys gave; they never left any room for discussion or fact-finding. In their minds, they knew who had killed the monkey and decided that the grasshoppers would pay for this deed.

"Oh, no," the grasshoppers kept repeating. "You are wrong. We did not kill your cousin!"

But the monkeys were deaf to their protests. "Yes, you did. You killed our cousin and you will pay for it!" they insisted.

Note: Reprinted from *Folk Stories of the Hmong: People of Laos, Thailand, and Vietnam* by Norma J. Livo and Dia Cha ©1991 Libraries Unlimited.

"Well then, if you are determined to fight," announced one grasshopper, "can we wait a little while to fight? It is so early in the morning and it is so cold. Why can't we wait until the sun comes up?"

After some group grumbling, the monkeys agreed to this, so they waited. The sun, as it usually does, rose high in the sky and warmed the grasshoppers on the hill. The fight began!

All of the monkeys grabbed big sticks and tried to hit the grasshoppers, but the grasshoppers just hopped onto their heads. When the monkeys struck at them, they hopped off, and of course, the monkeys kept hitting each other on the head as the grasshoppers just jumped away.

Bonk, bonk, bonk! The sound of clubs hitting monkey heads was heard everywhere on the hill. One monkey died from the club's blow; still, you could hear nothing but *bonk, bonk, bonk.*

After a while, all of the monkeys were dead except for one big one. He stood and looked around him at all of the dead monkeys. He was puzzled. "Look out now grasshoppers! I will catch you and eat you." And so, the remaining monkey snatched grasshoppers wherever he could, popped them into his snarling mouth, and crunched them. He snatched, ate, snatched, crunched, and snatched and ate. In fact, he ate so many grasshoppers that his stomach swelled and became tight as a drumhead.

A loud pop was heard as his stomach blew up from one grasshopper too many, and he gasped for breath as he fell. The battle was over. Who had won?

Jack and the Beanstalk
(England)

Once upon a time, there was a poor widow who had an only son named Jack, and a cow named Milky-white. All they had to live on was the milk the cow gave every morning, which they carried to the market and sold. But one morning, Milky-white gave no milk and they didn't know what to do.

"What shall we do, what shall we do?" asked the widow, wringing her hands.

"Cheer up, mother, I'll go and get work somewhere," said Jack.

"We've tried that before, and nobody would take you," said his mother. "We must sell Milky-white and with the money start shop, or something."

"All right, mother," said Jack. "It's market day today and I'll soon sell Milky-white and then we'll see what we can do."

So he took the cow's halter in his hand and started off. He hadn't gone far when he met a funny-looking old man who said to him, "Good morning Jack."

"Good morning to you," said Jack and wondered how the old man knew his name.

"Well, Jack, and where are you off to?" asked the old man.

"I'm going to market to sell our cow there."

"Oh, you look the proper sort of chap to sell cows," said the man. "I wonder if you know how many beans make five."

"Two in each hand and one in your mouth," replied Jack, just as sharp as a needle.

"Right you are," said the man. "And here they are, the very beans themselves," he continued, pulling out of his pocket a number of strange-looking beans. "As you are so sharp," he said, "I don't mind doing a swap with you—your cow for these beans."

"Go along," chuckled Jack. "Wouldn't you just like that?"

"Ah! You don't know what these beans are," said the man. "If you plant them overnight, by morning they grow right up to the sky."

"Really?" said Jack. "You don't say."

"Yes, that is so, and if it doesn't turn out to be true, you can have your cow back."

"Right," replied Jack, as he handed over Milky-white's halter to the man and pocketed the beans. Jack turned back toward home, and as he hadn't gone very far, it wasn't dusk by the time he got to his door.

"Back already, Jack?" asked his mother. "I see you haven't got Milky-white, so you've sold her. How much did you get for her?"

"You'll never guess, mother," answered Jack.

"No, you don't say so. Good boy! Five pounds, ten, fifteen, no, it can't be twenty."

"I told you, you couldn't guess. What do you say to these beans? They're magical. Plant them overnight and ... "

"What!" exclaimed Jack's mother. "Have you been such a fool, such a dolt, such an idiot, as to give away my Milky-white, the best milker in the parish, and prime beef to boot, for a set of paltry beans. Take that! Take that! Take that! And as for your precious beans, here they go out of the window. And now, off with you to bed. Not a sup shall you drink, and not a bit shall you swallow this very night."

So Jack went upstairs to his little room in the attic and sad and sorry he was, to be sure, as much for his mother's sake, as for the loss of his supper.

At last he dropped off to sleep.

When he woke up, the room looked so funny. The sun was shining into part of it, and yet all the rest was quite dark and shady. Jack jumped up, dressed himself, and went to the window. And what do you think he saw? The beans his mother had thrown out of the window into the garden had sprung up into a big beanstalk that went up, and up, and up, till it reached the sky. So the man had spoken the truth after all!

The beanstalk grew up quite close past Jack's window, so all he had to do was jump out onto the plant that ran upward, just like a big ladder. Jack climbed, and climbed, and climbed, and climbed, and climbed, until at last he reached the sky. And when he got there, he found a long, broad road going as straight as a dart. He walked along quite a way, till he came to a great big, tall house. On the doorstep, there was a great big, tall woman.

"Good morning, mum," said Jack, quite politely. "Could you be so kind as to give me some breakfast?" He hadn't had anything to eat the night before and was as hungry as a hunter.

"It's breakfast you want, is it?" said the great big, tall woman. "It's breakfast you'll be if you don't move off from here. My man is an ogre and there's nothing he likes better than boys broiled on toast. You'd better be moving on or he'll soon be coming."

"Oh! Please mum, do give me something to eat, mum. I've had nothing to eat since yesterday morning, really and truly, mum," begged Jack. "I may as well be broiled as die of hunger."

Well, the ogre's wife was not half so bad after all. She took Jack into the kitchen and gave him a hunk of bread and cheese and a jug of milk. Jack hadn't half finished these when *thump! thump! thump!* the whole house began to tremble with the noise of someone coming.

"Goodness gracious me! It's my old man," exclaimed the ogre's wife. "What on earth shall I do? Come along quick and jump in here." She bundled Jack into the oven just as the ogre came in.

He was a big one, to be sure. At his belt he had three calves strung up by the heels. He unhooked them, threw them down on the table and said, "Here, wife, broil me a couple of these for breakfast. Ah! What's this I smell?

"Fee-fi-fo-fum,
I smell the blood of an Englishman,
Be he alive, or be he dead
I'll have his bones to grind my bread."

"Nonsense dear," said his wife, "you're dreaming. Or perhaps you smell the scraps of that little boy you liked so much for yesterday's dinner. Here you go, and have a wash and tidy up and by the time you come back, your breakfast'll be ready for you."

Off the ogre went, and Jack was just going to jump out of the oven and run away when the woman stopped him. "Wait till he's asleep," she said. "He always has a doze after breakfast."

Well, the ogre had his breakfast, after which he went to a big chest and took out of it a couple of bags of gold. He sat down and continued to count till at last his head nodded and he began to snore, shaking the whole house.

Jack crept out of the oven on tiptoe, and as he was passing the ogre, he took one of the bags of gold under his arm and bolted off, till he came to the beanstalk. He threw down the bag of gold, which, of course, fell into his mother's garden. Then he climbed down and down, till at last he got home. He told his mother what had happened and showed her the gold. "Well mother," Jack said, "wasn't I right about the beans? They are really magical, you see."

So they lived on the bag of gold for some time, but at last they came to the end of it, and Jack decided to try his luck once more at the top of the beanstalk. He climbed, and climbed, and climbed, and climbed, and climbed, and climbed, till at last he came out onto the road again and up to the great big, tall house he had been to before. There, sure enough, was the great big, tall woman standing on the doorstep.

"Good morning, mum," said Jack as bold as brass. "Could you be so good as to give me something to eat?"

"Go away, my boy," said the big, tall woman, "or else my man will eat you up for breakfast. But aren't you the youngster who came here once before? Do you know, that very day, my man missed one of his bags of gold?"

"That's strange, mum," Jack replied. "I dare say I could tell you something about that, but I'm so hungry I can't speak till I've had something to eat."

Well, the big, tall woman was so curious that she took him in and gave him something to eat. He had scarcely begun munching it as slowly as he could when *thump! thump! thump!* they heard the giant's footsteps, and the wife hid Jack away in the oven.

All happened as it did before. In came the ogre, who said, "Fee-fi-fo-fum," and had his breakfast of three broiled oxen. Then he said, "Wife, bring me the hen that lays the golden eggs." When she brought it, the ogre said, "Lay," and it laid an egg all of gold. Then the ogre's head began to nod and he snored till the house shook.

Jack crept out of the oven on tiptoe, caught hold of the golden hen, and was off before you could say "Jack Robinson." But this time, the hen gave a cackle and woke the ogre. Just as Jack got out of the house, he heard him calling, "Wife, wife, what have you done with my golden hen?"

His wife said, "Why, my dear?"

That was all Jack heard, for he rushed off to the beanstalk and climbed down in record time! When he got home, he showed his mother the wonderful hen. Each time he said, "Lay," it laid a golden egg.

Even the hen that could lay golden eggs did not make Jack content. It wasn't very long before he determined to have another try at his luck at the top of the beanstalk. One fine morning, he rose up early, got onto the beanstalk, and climbed, and climbed, and climbed, and climbed, till he got to the top.

This time, he knew better than to go straight to the ogre's house. When he got near it, he waited behind a bush till he saw the ogre's wife come out with a pail to get some water. He crept into the house and got into the copper tub. He hadn't been there long when he heard *thump! thump! thump!* and in came the ogre and his wife.

"Fee-fi-fo-fum, I smell the blood of an Englishman," cried out the ogre. "I smell him, wife, I smell him!"

"Do you now, my dearie?" said the ogre's wife. "Then if it's that little rogue that stole your gold and the hen that laid the golden eggs, he's sure to have got into the oven." They both rushed to the oven, but luckily, of course, Jack wasn't there. The ogre's wife said, "There you are again with your fee-fi-fo-fum. Why, of course, it's the boy you caught last night that I've just broiled for your breakfast. How forgetful I am. How careless you are not to know the difference between live and dead after all these years."

So the ogre sat down to the breakfast and ate it. Every now and then, he would look around and mutter, "Well, I could have sworn ... " He would get up and search the larder and the cupboards and everywhere, only luckily, he didn't think of the copper tub.

After breakfast was over, the ogre called out, "Wife, wife, bring me my golden harp." She brought it and put it on the table before him. Then he said, "Sing!" and the golden harp sang most beautifully. It went on singing till the ogre fell asleep and commenced to snore like thunder.

Jack lifted up the copper lid quietly, got down like a mouse, and crept on hands and knees till he came to the table. He crawled up, caught hold of the golden harp, and dashed with it toward the door. The harp called out quite loudly, "Master! Master!" The ogre woke up just in time to see Jack running off with his harp.

Jack ran as fast as he could and the ogre came rushing after him. The ogre soon would have caught him, but Jack, who had a head start, knew where he was going and was able to dodge him. When he got to the beanstalk, the ogre was not more than twenty yards away. Suddenly, the ogre saw Jack disappear. Continuing down the road, the ogre came to the beanstalk and saw Jack underneath, climbing down for dear life.

The ogre didn't want to trust himself to such a weak ladder, so he stood and waited. Jack climbed down faster, as the harp cried out, "Master! Master!" Finally, the ogre couldn't stand it any longer and he swung himself down onto the beanstalk, which shook with his weight. Jack climbed down, down, down, with the ogre after him till he was very nearly home.

"Mother! Mother! Bring me an axe, bring me an axe," Jack called out. His mother came rushing out with the axe in her hand, but when she came to the beanstalk she stood stock still with fright, for there she saw the ogre with his legs just through the clouds.

Jack jumped down, got hold of the axe, and gave a chop at the beanstalk, cutting it in half. The ogre felt the beanstalk shake and quiver, so he stopped to see what was the matter. When Jack gave another chop with the axe, the beanstalk was cut in two and began to topple over. The ogre fell down and broke his crown, and the beanstalk came toppling after.

Jack showed his mother the golden harp. With showing that harp and selling the golden eggs, Jack and his mother became very rich. So rich, in fact, that later on he married a very beautiful princess. And, of course, they all lived happily ever after!

David and Goliath
(Old Testament, Judeo-Christian Bible)

Saul had been the king over Israel, but he had turned to evil. The Lord told Samuel that he would show him who had a heart that was worthy to be king. And so it was that Jesse was asked by Samuel to bring his sons for him to view. Nine of Jesse's sons were considered, but not chosen.

"Do you have any other children, Jesse?" Samuel asked.

"There is my youngest. He keeps the sheep," replied Jesse.

"Send and fetch him for consideration," commanded Samuel.

And so came a youth with ruddy face, who was goodly to look upon, named David. Samuel took the horn of oil and anointed David as worthy to be king.

Saul, who had lost his faith and worthiness, asked his servants to bring him a mighty, valiant man who could play the harp—a man of war; prudent, yet comely. Jesse answered the messengers of Saul and brought David to him. Saul was refreshed when he heard the music David called from his harp. The melody cleansed Saul of his evil spirit and he once again was a follower of the Lord.

An enemy army gathered to fight the Israelites. This army, the Philistines, stood on one side of the mountain facing the army of Israel on the other side, with the valley between them. The Philistines sent out their champion named Goliath. Goliath was a giant, wore a helmet of brass, and was armed with a coat of mail. The weight of the coat was 5,000 shekels of brass. He had brass guards on his legs and a target of brass that he carried. His spear had a staff that was like a weaver's beam. The spearhead itself weighed 600 shekels of iron.

This massive warrior cried out to the army of Israel. "Choose a man among you and let him come down to me. If he is able to fight with me and to kill me, then we will be your servants. However, if I kill him and win, then you shall be our servants and serve us." He continued, "I defy the armies of Israel this day! Give me such a man that we may fight."

Saul and all the men of Israel were dismayed with this and greatly afraid. They had no such champion. David had gone to feed his father's sheep and while he was there, Goliath presented himself every morning and evening for forty days.

David was called back from caring for his father's sheep. He returned to the battlefield and saw and heard Goliath calling out his challenge. David saw the fear held by the army of Israel and spoke to the men near him, "What shall be done to the man that killeth this Philistine and takes away the shame of Israel?"

Saul heard of David's question and sent for him. "Let no man's heart fail because of Goliath," said David. "Your servant will go and fight with this warrior."

Saul looked upon David and said, "I will give my elder daughter to you as wife. All I ask is that you be valiant and fight." David was humbled by this offer to be the son-in-law of the king. However, he favored another of Saul's daughters. Saul agreed that this daughter should be his, but David still felt unworthy, "I am a poor man. I have earned no honors."

Saul told David that, "I desire no dowry. Being poor is not of concern to me."

"I have no sword or weapons with which to fight," David stated. Saul gave David his armor, put a helmet of brass upon his head, and also armed him with a coat of mail. However, David removed all the clothing of a warrior and instead took his shepherd's staff and went to a brook where he chose five smooth stones. He put these in a shepherd's bag and held his sling in his hand. He approached Goliath.

Goliath came toward David and saw that David disdained him. He wore no battle gear nor carried a shield. What Goliath saw was a youth, ruddy and of a fair countenance, and he cursed him. "Come to me and you will be food for the fowls of the air and the beasts of the field."

As they met for battle, David put his hand to his bag and took out a stone, put it in his slingshot and aimed at Goliath's head. The stone struck Goliath in his forehead and sunk into it. With a crash, Goliath fell upon his face to the earth. And so it was that a youth, armed only with stones and sling, bested the giant boasting champion of the enemies of Israel.

The Magic Knot
(Peru)

Some who knew the lad named Borac said that he was the son of a king, while others said that he might not be. No one really ever knew. It was a wise old woman who lived nearby that said he was the son of a king. Since her stories were usually found to be true, people believed her. This is what she said of Borac:

A man who was gathering fruit by the side of a lake saw what he thought was a shining white stone. When he walked up to inspect it further, he found that it was a basket, neatly made of silk grass and lined with soft white feathers. In this nest, warm and cozy, the man found the baby Borac. "Ah, what have we here?"

The man took the basket and the baby home with him. His wife and three children were delighted with the baby. From the day the man found Borac, things went very well for him and he seemed to have nothing but good luck. Borac was treated exactly like the rest of the children and over time grew strong and handsome, with a ruddy face.

Borac's new family now had two boys and two girls. They played together every day and life was full of joy. There was a difference, though, because Borac seemed to see things and know things that the other children missed. The family lived at the foot of the mountains where the air was clean and sharp. All of the children had good eyesight and observed things at a distance as if they were looking through field glasses.

As Borac grew, he saw beauty in common things and pointed them out to the others. He took delight in showing them the lovely colors in the sunset sky, the pure blue of the lake water, the sparkling diamonds of the sun on the stream, and the fresh patches of green grass on the hills.

The songs of the birds were music that the other youngsters had grown up with and heard so often that they forgot the beauty of it. One day, Borac began to call like a bird, and from every tree and bush came a chorus so rich and wonderful that the joy in their hearts could be felt.

There was a special place high in the mountains, where the cliff ran straight up and was so smooth that no one had ever climbed it, even though the children were as sure-footed as goats. Halfway up this cliff was a broad ledge on which a condor had built its nest. Borac and the others often played at the foot of the cliff and enjoyed watching the condor drop off of his rock shelf with spread wings to float far above. There, the condors would wind in mighty circles for hours, floating higher and higher into the sky without wing motion. It seemed that they just leaned over and were swept up with the wind, up and up, until the birds looked no bigger than a hummingbird against the blue sky. In fact, some of them seemed to fly so high that they disappeared. The children knew that if they were granted a wish, it would be that they might have the power to soar and wheel like the great bird in the sky. They wanted to sweep up in a great curve, hang in the air, then float downward as if they were sliding, only to sweep up again at will.

One day, when the four children were there, one of the girls called out in great trouble. She pointed up to a cranny on the face of the cliff. The children saw two staring eyes of a large, mottled owl perched on a point of rock, just below which they could make out a dove on its nest. The little girl said the owl seemed to be screaming, "Ah! I see you, little dove. Sharp as needles are my claws. Sharp too, is my beak to tear you, and little owls are hungry for the flesh of doves."

That seemed dreadful to the children, and they began to shout and throw stones, trying to chase the owl away. It was no use. The nest of the rock dove was too far away and the face of the rock too smooth and sheer for any of them to climb. There seemed to be nothing they could do but watch until the little bird was caught. The dove was in great fear, but in spite of the danger, it stayed on the nest.

As for the owl, he turned his face downward toward the children. He heard their noise and as he looked at them, they could see his cruel eyes and his head feathers that were like horns. The owl gave no sign of leaving. He hooted and seemed to say, "Who cares for you, you little earth creatures?"

To the young watchers, it was like a jailer hanging over a prisoner who was innocent. Borac said, "It looks like a cruel man with a sword about to deal a death blow to a helpless child." The dove was helpless and above her, the owl was ready to swoop down at any moment.

Borac was so full of grief at what he saw that he started to climb the cliff. It seemed like a hopeless task, but he managed to climb a small way up. As he was doing this, a wonderful thing happened. From the sky where the condor wheeled, a long wing feather dropped. The condor had plucked this feather and it floated down, spinning and spinning, until at last it came to rest on a little rough rock close to Borac's right hand. As Borac picked the feather up with his right hand, he continued to clutch to the rock above his head with his left hand.

In a dangerous situation like this, why did Borac expend the effort to gather up the feather? He needed both hands to climb! After he grasped the feather, Borac looked at it curiously, as though he needed to admire its beauty. As he examined it, he twisted the feather just a bit, turning it with his fingers. And then, before the shocked and amazed eyes of the other three children, Borac floated gently from the face of the rock, out from the cliff and into the air, until he was poised over their heads.

Borac seemed to hang there as lightly as a piece of thistledown. When he twisted the feather again, just a little, he went upward. Borac tried other things, such as pointing it toward the face of the cliff, and he floated in that direction. "There is magic in the feather," he called down to the others. Saying that, he darted up as swiftly as the swiftest bird, rushing through the air and then swooping away from the cliff. He did this with such grace. Next, he went upward again, made a great circle, and dived. Finally, he shot upward, to the place where the owl sat.

When he did this, the sharp-clawed bird raised its wings and softly flew away, never to be seen again. Meanwhile, the three at the foot of the cliff were not at all frightened; they knew everything would end up right. In fact, they leaped with joy and delight. When they saw Borac standing on the rock ledge, they clapped their hands. The little slate-colored dove cooed with gratitude when the owl vanished.

Borac stooped and picked up something, but the children couldn't tell what it was. Behind the dove's nest, he saw a coil of silky stuff no thicker than a fine thread. In the middle of it was a queer knot. At first, he thought it was a part of the nest, and he did not touch it. However, the bird rose from its nest, picked up the end of the thread, and hopped with it to Borac.

He took it then, wound it up into a coil, and lay it in his hand. There it took up no more room than would a wild cherry. Its texture was extremely fine. Borac had heard the old woman speak of a magic knot that could bind evil things, even though they were strong enough to lift rocks.

No one knew how the magic knot got there, but it didn't matter very much. If it hadn't been for the knot, the owl would have captured the dove. Borac thought the condor may have known about the knot, for condors are very wise, travel great distances, and are able to see many things that escape the eyes of people. Borac did not stay long; with feather in hand, he leaped into the air and swooped down to land lightly on the earth near his companions.

Of course, there were many experiments. Each of the children took a turn flying with the feather. They had such fun as they flew higher and higher, and as they grew braver and braver. Each one of them had managed to stand on the far-away shelf near the condor's nest. They all found it easy to do.

The truth was that the magic feather would carry them quite safely as long as they believed in it. If they did not believe in it, they didn't budge from the earth. The children did not know what good the thread with its wonderful knot might be, but they knew it was certainly magic. So they guarded it carefully, packing it away in a nutshell where it would be handy when needed.

The magic knot was useful much sooner than they expected. One night, in a neighboring village, something happened. Some people were sitting and talking in a little house that sat near a clearing. When one of them became thirsty, he asked the boy of the house to take the gourd and go to the stream for some water.

Since the stream was just 100 yards away from the house, the boy went, bravely in the dark. The people in the house waited, and waited, and waited. They wondered why the boy was taking so long, and finally they went to look for him. Down to the little river they went and back again. There was no sign of the boy! That was bad enough, but on the next night, another boy went to visit a friend who lived five houses away and never arrived. The boy's father and mother went to look for him and traced his footsteps in the sandy road. They came to a place where the steps stopped and the road ahead was nothing but smooth sand.

Then on the third night, something else happened. After a girl and her sister were visiting, the younger girl started to go home alone. No sooner had she left than her sister, remembering how the boys had vanished, ran after her to keep her company. The night was moonless and a thin, cold mist hid the stars, but the girl could see her sister's white dress a little way ahead.

She could not see very plainly because it was so dark, but there was no mistake about it. The fluttering white dress was in front, cloudy looking, but there. Then—all of the sudden—something happened. The white cloud that was a dress vanished. The older sister ran to the place and heard a voice calling. The sound seemed to come from above her head. She looked up and saw a flutter of white for just an instant, then nothing more. Her sister had vanished, just like bubbles disappear.

With all of these strange happenings, there was terror in the village. During the day, villagers were nervous enough, but at night there was terror. No one dared to stir out after sunset. Even inside, people sat as if they were sitting on uncomfortable thorns.

Then, one night when there was no glimmer of light in the sky, a family sitting in a house heard a great tearing sound, as if some giant hand was pulling at the thatched roof. The light in the house went out and they sat in the room crouched, trembling, crowding close to one another. Their hearts throbbed. When at last it was quiet again they saw that there was a ragged hole in the roof. On the earthen floor there was a mark like the claw of a great bird. That was all. The hearts of the people were troubled.

Borac heard of all of these strange happenings and listened carefully. So did the wise old woman, who was there. She nodded thoughtfully and said, "Have no fear. Things will not go ill while the moon shines." She said much more, but particularly she asked Borac, "Do you have the magic knot?" Then she told him what to do. With the growing moon, the trouble ceased.

Meanwhile, Borac was busy. The old woman had talked with him, and day after day with the help of his magic feather, he made great flights. He circled high in the sky, crossed valleys, passed over mountains and lakes, and found strange lands far to the west. He came upon the great ocean that reached so far out it touched the sky.

The condors were good to Borac, and he flew with them, hither and thither. They flew fast and high and never tired. They took him in a new direction, to a place where a monstrous black bird rose out of a great, bare valley. The bird was so strong it could bear a llama in each claw and another in its beak. A condor beside it seemed to be tiny. Not only was it big, it was ugly. It had heavy-lidded eyes and sharp claws. When it flapped its wings, the wind from them caused the trees nearby to bend their tops, as if they leaned to whisper to each other.

Borac knew at once that it was a great bird of evil that swooped down on dark nights and carried men away. He also knew that there was only one and that it had laid just one egg. Borac watched for many days, and followed the bird wherever it went. At last he discovered its foul, messy nest high up in the mountains where people never went. By the side of the nest, in which there was an egg that was so huge a goat might have hidden in the shell of it, was a hole in the rock. In this hole, which had very steep sides, were all those creatures the great bird had carried away.

Day by day, Borac watched as the bird dropped fruit down into the hole for the unhappy creatures to eat until the egg was hatched. He knew that the people would be taken out and fed to the young bird one at a time. When the great bird had flown away, Borac ventured close to the hole and called out to the people, "Stay strong. You will be rescued soon. I will also kill the bird. Stay strong."

Borac flew back to his own place with his magic feather and told everyone what he had seen. Just as the wise old woman advised, Borac and his friends chose a stout tree and cut the top and the branches from it. Then they formed the trunk into the shape of a youth, leaving the roots fast in the earth. They painted this figure, and covered it with clothes. In its hand, they put a large gourd so that from afar it looked like someone going for water. Close to it, they built a house of poles and covered it with a roof of grass. They had everything ready before the moon was again dark.

Borac went into the house and waited for three nights. Then he took his feather and flew here and there. At last he saw a swiftly moving great black cloud, and knew this was the evil bird. He went back to his house and soon thereafter heard a great tearing sound in the air. As the bird came, it set up a terrific screeching and the noise of its beating wings was like thunderclaps. Down it swooped on the man of wood. Its claws were outstretched and its beak open. It seized the figure the next moment and was trying to lift it.

The more the figure resisted, the tighter the evil bird held, its claws and beak sunk fast in the wood. So fearsome were its struggles that the earth about the roots of the tree heaved. It seemed as if the roots would be torn out. Realizing that it could not move the thing, the bird tried to fly away, but its talons and beak were held fast by the wood, as if in a vise. All of its horrendous flapping and tearing was of no avail. Try as hard as it would, it could not release itself. Faster and harder it beat its wings and the wind from them bowed the bushes and shook the house in which Borac was hidden.

Then Borac came forth with the magic feather and magic knot. He was soon in the air above the struggling bird. He hovered there, unloosed the thread with the magic knot, and lowered it. Down it dropped, and soon it tangled in the beating wings. It looked like a web trapping a fly. Slight though the thread was, against the power of the magic knot, nothing could prevail. In a short time, the great black bird was bound helpless forever.

In the morning, Borac flew up to the nest in the far valley and floated down into the pit. One by one, he carried the unlucky people that the bird had caught from that place and returned them to their homes.

As for the egg, Borac put it on his shoulder and went to the ledge. There, he tumbled it over the edge, and it smashed to pieces as it fell. That was the end of the evil bird, which soon died. It was the very last of its evil kind. Today, all of the birds of the air have agreed never to harm people.

Thoughts About the Stories, Discussions, and Activities

THREE BILLY GOATS GRUFF

This well-known nursery tale provides us with a context in which to easily evaluate bullies and the bully syndrome.

- ⊙ *Trolls are common characters in Scandinavian folklore. Find other stories about trolls; are they always portrayed as bullies? Research in the library and on the Internet to find images of trolls, then create an illustration for this story that includes a troll.*
- ⊙ *What happens when one bully meets another? What kind of world would we have if everyone was a bully? Draw on personal experiences to write about this topic.*

BASKET WOMAN

This story is just another example from folktales of the bullies that are out in the world seeking to terrorize others.

- ⊙ *There are many folktales that contain characters like Basket Woman, who terrorize little children (e.g., Baba Yaga from Russia, and the Bogeyman from eastern Europe). Discuss reasons why there are so many stories of this type.*
- ⊙ *Are there adults who you feel frightened of—perhaps someone in the news or someone you see, but don't know very*

well? What is it about these people that makes you scared? Are they bullies? How does bullying relate to trustworthiness? Discuss this topic.

THE MONKEYS AND THE GRASSHOPPERS

This tale touches on the "might-makes-right" theory. The monkeys, being bigger and stronger, have no idea that the weaker, smaller grasshoppers could possibly vanquish them.

- *The monkeys in this story looked for someone to blame when they found their dead brother. This is called "scapegoating." Can you think of instances when groups of people have unfairly scapegoated another group or an individual? Discuss why scapegoating is so often done, and ways that it can be stopped.*
- *Do people who are bigger and stronger always win? Think of examples from your own life or from history where the smaller, weaker ones won. What made them succeed? Write an essay on "real winning."*

JACK AND THE BEANSTALK

This is another story that can be read on many different levels. Folk stories are populated with giants who are certainly not helpful, and they must be overcome. But Jack was not the perfect character either; and Mrs. Giant has a few loyalty/compassion conflicts.

- *It seems that everyone in this story does something wrong. Create a "wanted" poster for one of the characters, including an illustration and a list of the crimes they have committed.*
- *Make a list of and discuss some of the symbols in this story.*

DAVID AND GOLIATH

This Bible story featuring a giant takes a look at bullying and tells us about someone who believes in himself and through his confidence proves to be the victor.

- *Why are bullies so often depicted as giants in stories? Do bullies sometimes seem larger than they really are? How does David win against this bully? What character traits did he have that helped him? Make a list of and discuss qualities that are helpful in dealing with bullies.*

⊙ *The incident in this story is part of a battle. Is war a form of bullying or dealing with bullies? Can you think of any battles in recent times that involved bullying?*

THE MAGIC KNOT

In this tale, creatures of nature are bullies, but one unusual young fellow foiled the plot to kill. This is a *porquois* (or *how/why*) story that explains how something came to be the way it is.

⊙ *In this story, we see an owl as a bully, but owls are natural predators, which means they prey upon other creatures. Are predators really bullies? In the library or on the Internet, research owls and write a report about the different types and their habits.*

⊙ *Are there any instances in history where birds preyed on humans? In prehistoric times, there were large birdlike lizards called pterodactyls. What did they eat? Research and discuss these creatures.*

Other Activity Ideas

⊙ Bullying is aggressive behavior or intentional "harm-doing." It is carried out repeatedly and over time and is characterized by an imbalance of power. It can be physical or verbal. Examples of physical attacks include hitting, kicking, pushing, choking; verbal attacks include name-calling, threats, taunts, malicious teasing, rumors, and slander. Discuss what factors might contribute to someone becoming a bully.

⊙ Discuss how you can recognize and evaluate bullies at school.

⊙ Have you ever been a victim of or witnessed bullying? Have you ever felt like a bully? Write a short story about it without using real names.

⊙ Explore tactics that might be used to fend off bullies. Start with an incident such as when someone tells you your shirt is ugly. Make a list of ways to handle this situation. Did your list include such responses as making a joke of it and agreeing?

⊙ Some say that bullies are vying to get attention or power. How many ideas can you come up with to prevent or redirect their negative talents toward more positive pursuits?

⊙ Develop a program in which high school students visit elementary classrooms to discuss bullying. How can these discussion leaders influence the development of future bullies?

- *Conduct class meetings in which acceptable behavior is discussed. How can students be recognized for their positive behavior? Is there a way to achieve recognition by the entire school?*
- *Investigate community organizations and student groups that discuss bullying. What strategies do they promote that might be implemented in the schools?*
- *Invite a speaker from a local law enforcement group to discuss how violence in the family and how violent television programs may or may not contribute to youths becoming bullies.*
- *A study done by Dr. Dan Olweus in Bergen, Norway, found that children who bullied others were four times more likely than their peers to be convicted of crimes by the age of twenty-four. List some possible future implications of these findings.*
- *Author Mary Stolz wrote two books that concern bullies, in which the same events are considered from different viewpoints:* The Bully of Barkham Street *and* A Dog on Barkham Street *(published by Harper, 1960 and 1963, respectively). Find copies of these books at your library and share them. Compare and contrast character actions/reactions.*

  - *Does Martin, the bully in these books, compare to any school bullies you have known?*
  - *Write a play reflecting the characters and actions in these books, then role-play them.*

- *Can you think of any political/historical figures who were bullies (e.g., Hitler, Stalin)? Research in the library or on the Internet the life of one of these individuals and write about what may have contributed to his pathology.*
- *Consider the following ideas and use them to develop a program dealing with bullies and the bullied:*

  - *Know when, how, and from whom to get help.*
  - *Know when you should stand up to a bully and when you shouldn't.*
  - *Throw a bully off guard with humor.*
  - *Know how and when to avoid bullies.*

- *Role-play uses of humor to thwart a bully. Brainstorm responses and act them out.*
- *Discuss the options and actions involved in standing up to and confronting a bully when you see them bullying someone else.*

⊙ *Can you identify the following or any other suspicious behaviors among friends and schoolmates? (Parents also might want to consider these warning signs.) A youngster might be being bullied if he:*

  ⊙ *comes home from school with torn, damaged, or missing clothing, books, and belongings;*
  ⊙ *has unexplained bruises, injuries, cuts, and scratches;*
  ⊙ *seems isolated from peers and may not have a good friend to share time with;*
  ⊙ *appears to be fearful about attending school, walking to and from school, or riding the bus;*
  ⊙ *has poor appetite, headaches, and stomach pains (particularly in the morning);*
  ⊙ *chooses a longer, illogical route for going to and from school;*
  ⊙ *asks for or takes extra money from family;*
  ⊙ *appears anxious, distressed, unhappy, depressed, or tearful when returning home from school;*
  ⊙ *shows unexpected mood shifts, irritability, or sudden outbursts of temper;*
  ⊙ *has sleeping or eating problems;*
  ⊙ *loses interest in schoolwork and experiences a decline in academic performance;*
  ⊙ *talks about or attempts suicide.*

See the "General Activities" section at the end of this book for more ideas to further explore these topics.

General Activity Ideas

⊙ Prepare a story about an individual who exhibits good character to tell a small group. Possible sources include tales you have heard or read, ballads and musical lyrics, or stories you have researched. Like other families interested in preserving its history, your family has a cast of characters, traditions, and colorful events available. Collect and write some of these stories. Some questions to consider are:

  ⊙ How has history affected your family?
  ⊙ What treasures are stored in attics and other places?
  ⊙ Are there any stories in your family about how a great fortune was lost or almost made?
  ⊙ Interview family members about scars, physical or emotional, they might have—how did they get them?

⊙ Find an intriguing news item about issues of character in the newspaper. Use your imagination and write it into a full-blown story.

⊙ Can you predict future folk heroes or heroines? Use a current event and create a story about it and the characters involved. (Remember, "average" people are also rich sources for stories.)

⊙ Start a journal to document your storytelling activities. Look for storytelling events held at local schools, libraries, museums, or folklore societies. Make a note of the sources for the stories that you hear. Include copies of stories you tell and pictures of you telling them, along with any news items on story-telling. This journal could serve as a progress report of your story-telling activities. It can remind you of things that worked or did not work. Include some tips for telling stories. What did you find important?

- In a small group, brainstorm why storytelling is important. Make a list of these ideas.

- Select a familiar folktale (your school or public library contains many collections of folktales). Create symbols for each character and action. Using no text, "tell" the story with your symbols.

- Study the petroglyphs and petrographs that are found scratched or painted on rocks worldwide. Tree carvings can also be part of this method of communication. What stories can you develop to accompany these images of animals, birds, reptiles, monsters, and symbols of natural phenomena?

- What stories can you find about animals that have rescued people or other animals? Check newspapers, the Internet, and the library. Make a collection of these stories.

- Create bumper sticker slogans or posters to accompany one of the categories of values and character development presented in this book. Share them with others.

- Develop a crossword puzzle involving values and character development traits.

- Illustrate one of the stories in this book using one of a variety of media, such as pastels, chalk, oils, clay, collage, or acrylics. Share your images with others.

- Arrange one of the stories from this book for choral reading and select an instrumental piece to accompany it. Present the choral reading with the music playing in the background. (Older students may wish to perform this for younger students.)

- Write a sequel to one of the stories. Use your imagination. The new story can be an action-packed adventure, a romance, or even a comedy.

- After reading the stories, make a chart that compares and contrasts two of them. Look at the themes, characters, settings, and morals. Make a list of the differences and similarities.

- Illustrate one of the stories with a series of drawings. Cut the pictures apart, write the sequence number on the back of each one, and then mix them up. Tell the story to someone, give that person your pictures, and have him place them in the correct order. When he is done, the person you are sharing this with can use the sequence numbers on the back to self-check the order. (Mount the illustrations on poster board so they will be easier to handle and last longer.)

⊙ Develop a world map and show where the stories in the book take place.

⊙ Collect some fortunes from fortune cookies and use them to develop a story. Start it with a famous introduction, such as "it was a dark and stormy night."

⊙ There has been much controversy about the book Little Black Sambo. Analyze this story for attitudes you can discover in it. Should this book be censored? Discuss censorship and society concerns with participants. Could stories such as this be used in a positive way?

⊙ Collect samples of folk life and folklore, including:

  ⊙ oral traditions (spoken word, music, dance, and games),

  ⊙ material culture (tools, artifacts, fences, crafts and trades, folk art, and folk medicine); customs, beliefs, and rituals; festivals and drama, including religious and secular events (calendar events, feast days, market days, planting and harvest festivals, music and craft fairs, celebrations, and homecomings).

What do these ideas and things tell you about a culture and a time?

⊙ Writing Extensions:

  ⊙ Find or create a poem that could accompany one of the stories in this book.

  ⊙ Write a movie script for one of the stories. Perform the story and videotape the presentation.

  ⊙ Develop a puppet show using one of the stories.

⊙ Some of the common expressions of our language come from literature, for example: mad as a hatter, sour grapes, serendipity, goose that laid the golden egg, don't count your chickens before they're hatched, Cheshire grin, pay the piper, don't cry wolf, wolf in sheep's clothing, the Midas touch, open sesame, and Pandora's box. Can you think of others?

⊙ What are you afraid of? Do you remember what made you afraid? Were you able to get over some of your fears? If so, how did you accomplish this? Discuss this with others. Does talking about what you fear help you, or does it make things worse? (Sometimes, finding out that others have had fears about the same things can help relieve some of the intensity. When people think they are alone, fear has more power over them.)

- As a group, sift through some folk stories and analyze what fears the story characters cope with.
- Keep a file of stories that you find inspirational. Discuss what makes them inspirational to you.
- Identify story characters in familiar tales and books who are small, weak, and helpless. Do they change in the course of the story, and if so, how is this change identified? For instance, the Br'er Rabbit stories revolve around the character of a (usually considered) small, weak rabbit who succeeds because of his cleverness, not his size or strength.
- Visit a retirement community or a nursing home and collect stories that residents consider inspirational. What stories helped them overcome difficulties? The collected stories can be sorted into categories and published. After publication, share the stories with the folks in the nursing home or place a copy in the school library.
- What pieces of music do you find inspirational? As a group, develop a chart of these musical selections and categorize them according to their attributes. Do some pieces fit under several categories?
- Collect Charles M. Schultz's Peanuts comic strips. Analyze them, and list the ethical and value traits that are depicted. Why have these comics been popular for so long? Can they be helpful in solving problems?
- How could you help another student who is having problems in school?
- In a small discussion group, share about a time when you were caught telling a lie. Why did you tell the lie, what happened to you, and how did you feel? Write this story as it happened and then how you would have liked it to happen.
- Has anyone ever told you a lie? What did that lie make you feel like?
- Do all brothers and sisters get along? Share stories about some good times that you have had with your siblings.

  - What are some of the problems between brothers and sisters?
  - Brainstorm ways to solve problems between siblings.
  - Interview older relatives to find out their opinions of having brothers or sisters. Now that they are grown up, did their opinions change with age? If so, why?

- Ask your librarian or teacher for web-related addresses for pen pals. Research children who work, bear arms, starve, or are held as slaves. Discuss such topics with pen pals from other countries. Swap ideas with them about building worldwide tolerance and empathy. Share what you discover with others.

Bibliography

Bang, Molly Garrett. *Tye May and the Magic Brush*. Friday Harbor, WA: Turtleback, 1992.

Bennett, William J. *The Book of Virtues: A Treasury of Great Moral Stories*. New York, NY: Simon and Schuster, 1993.

Benninga, Jacques S., Editor. *Moral, Character and Civic Education in the Elementary School*. New York, NY: Teachers College Press, 1991.

Bolman, Lee G., and Terrence E. Deal. *Leading with Soul: An Uncommon Journey of Spirit*. San Francisco, CA: Jossey Bass, 1995.

Brooks, David, and Frank G. Goble. *The Case for Character Education: The Role of the School in Teaching Values and Virtues*. Northridge, CA: Studio 4 Productions, 1997.

Carter, Stephen L. *Integrity*. New York, NY: Harper Collins, 1996.

Chinen, Alan, M.D. *Beyond the Hero*. New York, NY: Jeremy P. Tarcher, 1993.

———. *In the Ever After*. Wilmette, IL: Chiron Publishers, 1989.

———. *Once upon a Midlife*. New York, NY: Tarcher, 1992.

Coles, Robert. *The Call of Stories: Teaching and the Moral Imagination*. Boston, MA: Houghton Mifflin, 1989.

———. *The Moral Life of Children*. Boston, MA: Houghton Mifflin, 1986.

Damon, William. *Greater Expectations: Overcoming the Culture of Indulgence in America's Homes and Schools*. New York, NY: Free Press, 1996.

DeRoche, Edward F., and Mary M. Williams. *Educating Hearts and Minds: A Comprehensive Character Education Framework*. Thousand Oaks, CA: Corwin Press Inc., 1998.

DeVries, Rheta, and Betty Zan. *Moral Classrooms, Moral Children: Creating a Constructivist Atmosphere in Early Education*. New York, NY: Teachers College Press, 1994.

Edwards, Carolyn Pope. *Promoting Social and Moral Development in Young Children*. New York, NY: Teachers College Press, 1986.

Frymier, Jack, et al. *Values on Which We Agree*. Bloomington, IN: Phi Delta Kappa, 1995.

Goleman, Daniel. *Emotional Intelligence: Why It Can Matter More than IQ*. New York, NY: Bantam, 1995.

Himmelfarb, Gertrude. *The Demoralization of Society: From Victorian Virtues to Modern Values*. New York, NY: Alfred A. Knopf, 1995.

Jackson, Philip W., Robert E. Boostrom, and David T. Hansen. *The Moral Life of Schools*. San Francisco, CA: Jossey Bass, 1993.

James, Edward T., Editor. *The American Plutarch: 18 Lives Selected from the Dictionary of American Biography*. New York, NY: Charles Scribner's Sons, 1964.

Kidder, Rushworth M. *How Good People Make Tough Choices: Resolving the Dilemmas of Ethical Living*. New York, NY: Fireside (Simon and Schuster), 1996.

Kilpatrick, William. *Why Johnny Can't Tell Right from Wrong: Moral Literacy and the Case for Character Education*. New York, NY: Simon and Schuster, 1992.

Kilpatrick, William, Gregory Wolfe, and Suzanne M. Wolfe. *Books that Build Character: A Guide to Teaching Your Child Moral Values Through Stories*. New York, NY: Simon and Schuster, 1994.

Kirschenbaum, Howard. *100 Ways to Enhance Values and Morality in Schools and Youth Settings*. Needham Heights, MA: Simon and Schuster, 1995.

Kohlberg, Lawrence. *Essays on Moral Development: The Philosophy of Moral Development*. Volume I. San Francisco, CA: Harper and Row, 1981.

———. *Essays on Moral Development: The Psychology of Moral Development*. Volume II. San Francisco, CA: Harper and Row, 1984.

Leming, James S. *Character Education: Lessons from the Past, Models for the Future*. Camden, ME: The Institute for Global Ethics, 1993.

Lickona, Thomas. *Educating for Character: How Our Schools Can Teach Respect and Responsibility*. New York, NY: Bantam, 1991.

———. *Raising Good Children from Birth Through the Teenage Years*. Toronto, Ontario: Bantam, 1985.

Lickona, Thomas, Editor. *Moral Development and Behavior: Theory, Research and Social Issues*. New York, NY: Holt, Rinehart and Winston, 1976.

Livo, Norma J. *Celebrating the Earth: Stories, Experiences, and Activities*. Englewood, CO: Libraries Unlimited, 2000.

———. *Story Medicine: Multicultural Tales of Healing and Transformation*. Englewood, CO: Libraries Unlimited, 2001.

———. *Troubadour's Storybag: Musical Folktales of the World*. Golden, CO: Fulcrum, 1996.

———. *Who's Afraid . . . ? Facing Children's Fears with Folktales*. Englewood, CO: Libraries Unlimited, 1994.

Livo, Norma J., and George O. Livo. *The Enchanted Wood and Other Tales from Finland*. Englewood, CO: Libraries Unlimited, 1999.

McDermott, Gerald. *The Stone-Cutter*. New York, NY: Viking Press, 1975.

Molnar, Alex, Editor. *The Construction of Children's Character: The Ninety-sixth Yearbook of the National Society for the Study of Education*. Chicago, IL: University of Chicago Press, 1997.

Morley, Christopher. *Modern Essays*. "The Fifty-First Dragon" by Heywood Broun. New York, NY: Harcourt Brace, 1921.

Murphy, Madonna M. *Character Education in America's Blue Ribbon Schools: Best Practices for Meeting the Challenge*. Lancaster, PA: Technomic Publishing Co., 1998.

Noddings, Nel. *Caring: A Feminine Approach to Ethics and Moral Education*. Berkeley, CA: University of California Press, 1986.

Piaget, Jean. *The Moral Judgment of the Child*. New York, NY: The Free Press, 1965.

Pipher, Mary. *The Shelter of Each Other*. New York, NY: G. P. Putnam's Sons, 1996.

Reimer, Joseph, D.R. Paolitto, and R.H. Hersh. *Promoting Moral Growth: From Piaget to Kohlberg*. New York, NY: Longman, 1983.

Sockett, Hugh. *The Moral Base for Teacher Professionalism*. New York, NY: Teachers College Press, 1993.

Strike, Kenneth A., and P. Lance Ternasky, Editors. *Ethics for Professionals in Education: Perspectives for Preparation and Practice*. New York, NY: Teachers College Press, 1993.

Trelease, Jim, Editor. *Hey! Listen to This: Stories to Read Aloud*. New York, NY: Penguin Books, 1992.

Vincent, Philip Fitch. *Promising Practices in Character Education: Nine Success Stories from Around the Country*. Chapel Hill, NC: Character Development Group, 1996.

Wiley, Lori Sandford. *Comprehensive Character-Building Classroom: A Handbook for Teachers*. Manchester, NH: Character Development Foundation, 1997.

Wilson, James Q. *The Moral Sense*. New York, NY: Free Press, 1993.

———. *On Character: Essays by James Q. Wilson*. Washington, DC: The AEI Press, 1995.

Wynne, Edward, and Kevin Ryan. *Reclaiming Our Schools: A Handbook on Teaching Character, Academics and Discipline*. New York, NY: Merrill, 1997.

INTERNET RESOURCES

http://www.ethicsusa.com (character education).

http://www.character.org (character education).

http://www.indiana.edu/~eric_rec/ieo/bibs/characte.html (support for character education).

http://www.cde.ca.gov/character/biblio1.html (character education in California).

http://www.ethics.org/character (National Institute for Character Education).

http://www.useekufind.com/tresourc.htm (research on violence in the public schools).

http://www.learning-for-life.org (social and life skills).

www.everythingnick.com (talking with kids about tough issues).

www.siecus.org (issues related to sexuality).

www.loveandlogic.com (parenting topics).

www.canwetalk.org (National Education Association offers information on its parent-child communication training program).

www.tentalks.com (information about a parent-child communication training program).

http://coach.dosomething.org (provides details on special class curricula).

www.glef.org (The George Lucas Educational Foundation, Sara Armstrong, Ph.D., Director of Content, P. O. Box 3494, San Rafael, CA 94912, phone 415-444-8912, saarmst@glef.org. This organization is searching out educational programs that are unique and will contribute to the field of education).

http://jama.ama-assn.org (a source for information on bullying. The April 25, 2001 issue of the *Journal of the American Medical Association* reports on bullying in our schools.).

http://www.aap.org/advocacy/releases/disastercomm.htm (offers advice on communicating with children about disasters).

http://www.pbs.org/americaresponds/educators.html (America responds—classroom resources).

http://www.nasponline.org/NEAT/terror_eds.html (children and responding to national disaster information for teachers).

http://www.ag.uiuc.edu/~disaster/teacher/csndact2.html (stress, and natural disasters: school activities for children).

http://kidshealth.org/parent/positive/talk/news.html (how to talk to your child about the news).

ORGANIZATIONS

Character Education Partnership, 1600 K Street NW, Suite 501, Washington, DC 20006.

Reilly Center for Science, Technology and Values, 346 O'Shaughnessy Hall, University of Notre Dame, Notre Dame, IN 46556.

Index

Aesop, tales and stories from, 32, 33, 73, 74, 79, 169, 172
Africa, tales and stories from, 43–44, 70–72, 202–203
Ananzi and the Lion, 70–72, 81
Animals, role in stories with, 6. *See also specific animal*
Archetypal stories, 7
Arion and His Harp, 125–27, 145–46

The Badger's Money, 121–24, 145
The Bag of Gold, 96–98, 99–100
The Bagpiper and the Rats, 213–16, 223
The Bamboo Princess, 11–14, 22
Barrie, James, 37
Barron, Tom, 84
Basket Woman, 231–32, 250–51
Battle of Bannockburn, 41, 42
Bible, stories from, 19, 23, 241–42
Blue Willow, legend of, 17 n
The Boy Who Cried Wolf, 73, 81
Brothers Grimm, 133–34
Broun, Heywood, 106–112
The Bully of Barkham Street (Stolz), 254
Bullying, 2, 229–55
Bush, George W., 2
Byron, George Byron (Lord), 84

California, Native American story from, 144
Campbell, Joseph, 7, 85
Carrot Seed (Krauss), 116–17
Cha, Dia, 149
Character education, 1–3
China, tales and stories from, 15–17, 105
"Cinderella," stories of, 150, 224
Citizenship and civic virtues, 2–3
Colorado, tales and stories from, 204–206, 217–19
Columbine School, 2
Coyote, 178–79, 217–19
Coyote and Fox, 217–19, 223
The Crane and the Wood Grouse, 180, 192

David and Goliath, 241–42, 251–52
The Deer of India, 141–43, 147
The Delicious Strawberry, 29, 34
Dinesen, Isak, 7
A Dog on Barkham Street (Stolz), 254
The Donkey in the Lion's Skin, 74, 81
The Dragon and the Prince, 45–50, 57

England, tales and stories from, 235–40
The Escape of the Pigeons, 173–74, 191

Ethics education, 2–3
Ethiopia, tales and stories from, 43–44

Fables, 6–7
The Fifty-First Dragon, 106–112, 114–15
Find Where the Wind Goes: Moments From My Life (Jemison), 84
Finland, tales and stories from, 92–95, 96–98, 180
Folk Stories of the Hmong: Peoples of Laos, Thailand and Vietnam (Livo and Cha), 149
Folktales, as models of behavior, 4–7
The Fox and the Horse, 133–34, 146
France, tales and stories from, 220–22

Germany, tales and stories from, 51–55, 133–34, 213–16
The Glencoe Massacre, 75–78, 81–82
Gloria Barron Young Heroes Prize, 84
The Golden Lion, 135–40, 146
Goldsmith, Martin, 25
"The Good Samaritan," 19, 23
The Grateful Foxes, 128–32, 146
The Great Canoe, 175–77, 191
Greece, tales and stories from, 125–27
Guinness Book of Records, 59

Healing Well, 201, 207
"The Hero's Adventure" (1988), 85
Hmong, tales and stories from, 149, 233–34
Horace, 37
The Hummingbird, 105, 114
The Hunt, 172, 190–91

India, tales and stories from, 141–43
The Inextinguishable Symphony (Goldsmith), 25
Intelligence and Luck, 197–200, 207
Internet, resource of, 3
Iowa, Native American story from, 18
Italy, tales and stories from, 135–40

Jack and the Beanstalk, 235–40, 251
Japan, tales and stories from, 11–14, 30–31, 121–24, 128–32
Jefferson, Thomas, 3
Jemison, Mae, 84
Journals, 36

Kalavela, epic of, 5

"Kindness and Justice Challenge," 2–3
King, Martin Luther, Jr., 3
Kipling, Rudyard, 193
Korea, tales and stories from, 89–91
Krauss, Ruth, 116–17

Lessons from a Father, 170–71, 190
Lincoln, Abraham, 83
The Lion and the Mouse, 169, 190
Little Black Sambo, 259
The Little Red Hen, 153–54, 163
Long, Broad, and Sharpsight, 181–89, 192
The Lovers in Spirit Lake, 18, 23
Lovers in the Sky, 15–17, 23
The Lute Player, 63–66, 80

The Magic Fish of Gold, 92–95, 99
The Magic Knot, 243–49, 252
The Man Who Roared, 204–206, 208
Maori, tales and stories from, 175–77
The Monkey and the Dolphin, 79, 82
The Monkeys and the Grasshoppers, 233–34, 251
Moyers, Bill, 85
Music, influences of, 36–37

Native Americans, tales and stories from, 7, 18, 144, 162, 178–79, 217–19, 231–32
Navajo, importance of stories of, 7
New Testament, parable from, 19, 23
New Zealand, Maori tale from, 175–77
North America, tales and stories from, 18, 144, 162, 231–32
Norway, tales and stories from, 229–30

Old Badger and Old Frog, 144, 147
Old Testament, story from, 241–42
Olweus, Dan, 254
Oregon, Native American tale from, 178–79

Paiute, tales and stories from, 162
The Parable of the Good Samaritan, 19, 23
Parks, Rosa, 85
Peanuts, 260
Persia, tales and stories from, 173–74
Peru, tales and stories from, 243–49
Pied Piper of Hamlin, 223
Poland, tales and stories from, 45–50

Ralston, W. R. S., 7
Random Acts, 25
Random acts of kindness, 24–25
Robert the Bruce, the King, 41–42, 56
Russia, tales and stories from, 63–66

The Sage Grouse, 162, 164
Samaritan, parable of, 19, 23
School violence, 2
Scotland, tales and stories from, 20–21,
    41–42, 75–78, 113, 155–61, 201
Second Jungle Book (Kipling), 193
Seizing the Nettles, 113, 115
The Selkie, 20–21, 23
September 11, 2001, events of, 2, 37, 83,
    148
Shelley, Percy Bysshe, 37
Shue, Andrew, 2
Simms, Laura, 4
The Singing, Soaring Lark, 51–55, 57
Slavonic tales and stories, 67–69, 181–89,
    197–200
Southeast Asia, tales and stories from,
    233–34
Stealing Fire, 178–79, 191
Stolz, Mary, 254
The Stonecutter, 30–31, 34
Stories/storytelling, 3–7

The Storyteller, 43–44, 56–57

Teaching with Folk Stories of the Hmong
    (Cha and Livo), 149
Tennessee, story from, 170–71
Three Billy Goats Gruff, 229–30, 250
The Three Shirts of Bog Cotton, 155–61,
    163
Tiger's Whisker, 89–91, 99
Toads and Diamonds, 220–22, 224
The Town Mouse and the Country Mouse,
    33, 35
Two Friends, 202–203,
    207–208

United States, tales and stories from,
    153–54, 170–71, 204–206. *See also*
    Native Americans
Ute, tale from, 231–32

Values education, 1–3

Washington, George, 83
The Wind and the Sun, 32, 35
The Wonderful Hair, 67–69, 80

Zen Buddhists, tales and stories
    from, 29